The Oberammergau
Passion Play

The Oberammergau Passion Play

VERNON HEATON

Illustrated

ROBERT HALE · LONDON

© *Vernon Heaton 1970, 1979 and 1983*
First edition 1970
Second edition 1979
Third edition 1983

Robert Hale Limited
Clerkenwell House
Clerkenwell Green
London, EC1

ISBN 0 7090 1283 7

Printed in Great Britain by
Redwood Burn Limited
Trowbridge, Wiltshire
and bound by Hunter & Foulis Limited

To
Aidan Ronald Bruce

Contents

Illustrations

PICTURE CREDITS

Peter G. Wickman: 1, 14; Werner Gorter: 4, 16, 18; J. Allan Cash: 19; The Mansell Collection: 2, 7, 13, 17a, 17b, 17c, 17d; Monitor Press Features Ltd: 3; Paul Popper: 5, 6, 9, 15; Huber Photos: 8, 10, 11, 12a, 12b, 12c, 12d; Gemeinde Oberammergau: 25; Keystone: 22, 23, 24; Associated Press Ltd: 20, 21

1 Plagues and Passion Plays

Neither plagues nor Passion Plays are innovations of the past 1,000 years, nor is the one dependent on, nor in consequence of, the other.

Certainly Passion Plays, telling the story of the sufferings, the crucifixion and the resurrection of Christ, could not have preceded the event, but pestilence of one sort or another are believed to have spread their ugly tentacles across the face of the known world, in successive tides of slaughter, long before the dawn of Christianity.

Contagious diseases most assuredly persisted on the African continent long before records of any such scourges were kept. Certainly the physician Rufus of Ephesus declared, somewhere around A.D. 50, that bubonic plague had ravaged Egypt, Libya and Syria for centuries.

But there is no recorded history of the plague having crossed from Africa to the northern shores of the Mediterranean earlier than the sixth century A.D., though that inland sea had never been a bar to communication between the southern and northern continents since the first simple boats were launched, long before the Pharaohs ruled over Egypt.

But, as was to be expected, the first known cases of the plague in Europe occurred in the ports, brought there by African traders, slave crews from their ships and the rats that infested them. From there it moved steadily and disastrously through the coastal towns and villages and then turned inland, spreading its infectious horror far and wide over the Roman world of those days, over every, kingdom, principality and dukedom and eventually reaching the shores of Britain.

The Venerable Bede records an almost regular ten year high tide of pestilence as the plague ebbed and flowed over the whole of Europe. Each century thereafter felt the scourge at one time or another, and whole centres of population withered and died.

Probably the most disastrous plague ever to infect Europe washed over the continent in a black cloud of doom during the fourteenth century. It rolled northwards from the Adriatic to the Baltic, to Spain in the west and to Poland in the east. Historians of that era claim that as many as 25,000,000 people perished, almost two-thirds of the population of Europe.

Few who contracted the disease survived, and—as it had long been public knowledge that the sickness passed to almost everyone who came in contact with a diseased person, even before the diseased person knew that he was stricken—whole families would break up at the first hint of the approach of the plague. Others would bar their houses against intruders until hunger forced them out into the open, and then, when the Black Death penetrated their fastness at last, they would desert their sick, abandon the dead and leave the aged to fend for themselves in a mad, panic-stricken dash for safety, as far away as possible from the horror—which served only to spread the plague farther and farther afield.

Generally too, the authorities would panic and desert

their posts, leaving the citizens of their towns and villages to fend for themselves and to their fate. Some few brave souls, however, would coerce their fellow citizens into taking what precautions they could to hold back the tide of death. The dead would be consigned to great pits away from the houses, though few but the mental defectives and criminals could be compelled into undertaking the dreadful task of collecting the rapidly putrefying bodies in the 'dead carts' and taking them to the pestiferous pits. But too often the bodies would be left to rot in their beds, or in the streets, until such time as those of the scavengers who had not fled, made their sorry rounds.

Great fires were lit in all the open squares and the access roads, in the desperate hope that the flames would devour the germs and parasites as they were carried on the air— and a large number of buildings were destroyed in this fashion as many a householder attempted to ward off the plague by lighting oversize fires in his own home. And the inhabitants of every community who had not fled before the advancing pestilence would arm themselves with swords, cudgels, axes, or whatever else came to hand, in an urgent determination to stave off the hoardes of starving, already diseased refugees from the stricken areas.

But invariably the defences of each habitation would be breached, sooner or later, through unguarded side-streets and alleyways, causing yet another exodus as fresh waves of terrified people fled from their homes.

Further outbreaks of the plague occurred during the fifteenth, sixteenth and seventeenth centuries, despite the fact that it had long been common knowledge that the source of the dreadful disease lay in the filth and vermin that was permitted to infest the cities of Europe—and despite the tragic reminders brought to the attention of the authorities by each successive onslaught of the Black Death.

The practice of throwing garbage and other filth from the houses into the streets still persisted, creating dark clouds of glutinous flies and an appalling stench; wells continued to be choked and polluted by the carcases of decaying animals; rats and other vermin infested the houses; and the need for clean clothing and bodily hygiene was almost totally disregarded.

Under such conditions pestilence flourished, and the citizens of Europe, in those not so distant years, lived under an ever-present pall of fearful expectancy.

The mass of the people, uneducated and mostly apathetic, bowed their heads before each eddy of the plague, accepted the loss of relatives and friends—wives, husbands and children—with almost stoical indifference, and hoped, without much faith, that they would survive the next outbreak . . . and the next . . . and the next . . .

A few stout-hearted citizens took what precautions they could—keeping their homes free from rats, boiling the water they and their families drank and avoiding the over-crowded theatres, ale-houses and public markets—yet others sought immunity through the churches and in prayer.

Nor were Passion Plays the accepted form of 'Thanks be to God' rendered by every community that had been purged of the plague. Such performances were enacted at least as early as the eleventh century.

Religious plays—or 'Mysteries'—were written and produced at an even earlier date, telling stories of the Nativity, Passion and Resurrection of Christ. But, as they were generally written in Latin, they had little impact on the people. These Mysteries, were a progression from such pagan festivals as the Mithraic Feast of what is now called 'Christmas Day', and the Feast of Fools, which, in its turn, was probably a development of the Kalend Feasts.

Possibly the earliest form of Christian plays were those that began to appear during the fourth century, when choirs would sometimes chant in sections and make sufficient gestures to give a sound and sight story of some event in the life of Christ, or one of the saints, and present it during Mass on religious high days.

In the thirteenth century, Nativity and Epiphany Plays —stories of the 'Adoration of the Cross' and of the 'Suffering, Death and Resurrection of Christ'—became regular features of Good Friday and were perhaps the earliest 'true' versions of the 'Passion Plays', but it was not until the fourteenth century that such plays began to be written in the language of the country in which they were to be performed—and so transformed what had been for so long, a 'mystery' to the vast majority of the population into a more comprehensive story.

2 Oberammergau Before the Plague

Oberammergau lies deeply embedded in the Bavarian Alps, twelve and a half miles to the north of the Tyrolese border and some sixty-four miles to the south and west of Munich. The Ammer Valley in which it was for so long secreted, is 2,750 feet above sea level but forms a deep cutting through the Kofel range of the Alps. Peaks reach to over 6,000 feet on either side, and the Kofel Mountain itself dominates the southern end of the village to a height of 4,400 feet. Further to the south the Zugspitz, Germany's highest mountain, reaches skywards and can be seen from Oberammergau on a clear day. The River Ammer, which flows along the floor of the valley and through the village, has its source in the mountain springs of the Tyrol and empties itself into the Ammersee to the north.

The history of Oberammergau is often legendary, and in any event there are great gaps in the story. Long before the Christian era the Ammer Valley was inhabited by Celts, though we know little of them beyond the place names they left behind them. In fact it is probable that there was no real centre of population in the district, however small, until the Romans came to carve a road through the mountains as a supply route to their legions in the north. Relics of the Roman occupation are prolific: coins, weapons, pieces of armour and memorial stones have been unearthed to tell something of the tale of those distant years.

But with the decline of the Roman Empire and the withdrawal of their forces to the south, the story lapses and the Ammer Valley fades into obscurity.

We do know, however, that after the Romans left the Franks ravaged the whole of Bavaria, almost depopulating the region in their ruthless ferocity. We know too that in 696 Rupert, Bishop of Worms, introduced Christianity to the region and established several monasteries, and that St. Boniface arrived in Bavaria in about 734 to reinforce the new faith among a doubting people. We can be pretty certain that these events had some influence on the inhabitants of the Ammer Valley, but no details of it appear in the chronicles of those times. No doubt, with the passing of the Romans, and in consequence the cessation of much of the traffic on the through road built by them, the valley, sunk deeply and inaccessibly in its tiny cleft in the fastness of the Alps, must have lost what little importance it had had.

Not until the ninth century did the Ammer district emerge, briefly, into the light of history again when it came under the domination of the legendary Guelphs—a name that is still borne by some of the most powerful families in Europe to this day, and with whom even our own queen can claim kinship.

In that era the Guelphs owed allegiance to no man and were prone to hold their heads high in disdain of those who had the need to bow their heads to some overlord. But Heinrich, son of the ageing Duke Ethiko, greedy and ambitious, secretly acknowledged the suzerainty of the Emperor, Louis the Pious, in exchange for additional lands to add to the Guelph territories.

Ethiko was heartbroken when he learned of his son's failure to maintain the family's proud boast. He gathered together twelve of his most faithful followers and retired into the deep seclusion of the Ammer Valley, determined to have no further contact with the outside world. Duke Ethiko is reputed to have built a church in the valley, and in due time, to have been buried there, along with his followers—but no trace of the site can be found today.

Yet again the Ammer Valley fades back into the mists of obscurity—not to emerge for another 300 years.

In the twelfth century Frederick the Redbeard purchased the valley from the Guelphs. After that the Hohenstaufen family held it until Conradin died, to be succeeded by his uncle, Ludwig, Duke of Bavaria.

Ludwig's son, another Ludwig, was elected Emperor of Bavaria in 1314, and it was he who made the first of the sacred vows that so profoundly influenced the Ammer Valley and the tiny hamlet of Oberammergau—some 300 years before the plague and the second vow.

There are many legendary stories concerning the events that led up to the vow made by Ludwig the Bavarian, as the Emperor came to be called, and to the foundation of the monastery at Ettal, only a mile or two from Oberammergau. One avers that the Emperor, grateful for his release from embroilment in war during a visit to Italy, made a vow before a statue of the Virgin Mary in Rome, to build a monastery at the spot where he first set foot on Bavarian soil again.

Another version tells of the Emperor's pilgrimage to Rome and how, one day, while he was at prayer before a statue of the Virgin Mary, an old monk entered his cell through a locked door, presented him with a figurine of Mary and commanded him to return to Bavaria and there to found a monastery for the disciples of St. Benedict.

Both of these stories tells of how, after his return to Bavaria, Ludwig's horse carried him into a wilderness of forests and mountains, and there, before a spruce tree, the horse went down onto its knees three times in quick succession. Ludwig accepted this as a heaven-sent sign that this should be the site of the monastery he had vowed to build.

Could it have been that the horse, having been ridden far over rough tracks and mountain passes and then been called on to bear its heavy burden up the very steep ascent to what is now called Ettal, stumbled? Be the cause sheer exhaustion or an impulse from a more celestial source, Ludwig determined to build his monastery on the spot.

The site at Ettal straddles the ancient road built by the Romans and abandoned by them in the face of the advancing barbarians more than 1,000 years earlier, and it was along this road that many tons of Italian marble, used in the construction of the monastery, was hauled. The foundation stone was laid by the Emperor himself in 1330, and two years later many of the buildings were ready for use.

The centre-piece of the massive construction was a beautiful church, built of the white marble from Italy, and though the design was Gothic in character, it was built in a strange but supremely attractive, twelve-sided fashion and crowned by a dome that reached skywards to a point. Inside a circle of twelve chapels had been constructed, and on the high altar rested a statue of the Virgin Mary—who was declared to be the founder of the monastery.

In that year, as sufficient progress had been made, twenty Benedictine Monks took up residence and, on the orders of the Emperor, initiated a School for Knights.

Nearby, in the valley below Ettal, Oberammergau stood on the site of an old fortification, a defence against the marauding bandits who had infested the place after the Frankish invasion of the third century. Under its protection, no doubt the little village developed, slow and untroubled in the peaceful seclusion of the mountains—and it was from that source that Ludwig the Bavarian must have found much of the labour needed to build the Ettal Monastery. As a token of his gratitude for the work the villagers had done, the Emperor Ludwig granted them certain hereditary rights and privileges. He freed them from serfdom—the normal unhappy state of the peasants of those days. They were to be allowed to own their own homes, to be able to dispose of them as they wished, and to cultivate their own land for their own benefit—an outstanding piece of liberalism in an era when peasants and their 'property' was owned, 'body, soul, timber and soil', by their overlords.

Ludwig granted the villagers the sole right to provide the teams of horses needed to haul the heavy drays and the coaches of the merchants up the steep ascent to Ettal, and to draw them as far as the main road at Schongau to the north and to Partenkirchen to the south.

Until then Oberammergau had been of little commercial account. Though its inhabitants had probably been quietly content with their seclusion from the world of wars, tax collectors and the persistent demands of landowners, their standard of living must have bordered on the poverty line. Remote from markets, industry could have been of little consequence, with few visitors from the outside world, there must have been little knowledge of the opportunities of employment beyond the valley and, because of the paucity of farming in the district, almost no demand for their labour. Nor, because of the steep, heavily wooded foothills of the surrounding mountains and the stony nature of the ground in the valley, could the cultivation of the soil have provided more than enough provender to satisfy the needs of each individual farmer and his family.

But now that the new monastery at Ettal had begun to

attract a regular flow of pilgrims, and the merchants had begun to diverge from the main roads between the ports of Italy and the cities to the north in order to see this already famous shrine, a measure of prosperity began to rise in the Ammer Valley.

By 1340 the monastery was renowned far beyond the Bavarian frontiers, and, because of the hospitality it was reputed to offer, it drew an ever-increasing stream of visitors, until the mountain pass became a flourishing trade route—where none but the citizens of Oberammergau had the right to harness their teams of horses to the heavy wagons of the merchants, to draw them over the steep access road to Ettal and through the valley.

And with the rapidly growing demand for ancillary services, warehouses began to spring up in which the merchants could store their wagons and wares, and, alongside them, repair shops, eating houses and shops were established. Trading centres were opened up in the village too, so that the craftsmen of Oberammergau could display and sell their products to the merchants, who, in their turn and at considerable profit to themselves, could dispose of them in the cities, far beyond the confines of the remote valley.

With no overlord to soak them of their newfound wealth and in the hope of preserving their unexpected prosperity, the elders of Oberammergau, in their wisdom, began to enforce a disciplined code of conduct on their fellow citizens. A Guild of Teamsters was formed, trading practises were laid down, and the long established art of woodcarving was encouraged as a viable industry.

No clue is given in recorded history of the origin of the woodcarving craft in Oberammergau; perhaps it grew up as a way of easing the burden of boredom caused by the long, bitterly cold winters. Almost the first flurry of snow would put an end to work on the land or in the forests, and within a matter of days the snow would lie so deep that only the few paths in the village itself would be kept open. And inevitably, the villagers would become house-bound and huddled around their fires.

With reading an art beyond the knowledge of the ordinary citizen, and reading matter in any case probably non-existent in the village; with no form of entertainment other than the music to be obtained from the few instruments they made for themselves, and no teachers to occupy their minds, boredom could only have been offset by some form of manual occupation that needed little space, a minimum of tools and readily available materials on which to work.

Surrounded by dense forests and stacks of cut timber for the winter fires, the answer to that problem must have been self-evident, and no doubt it had long ago become the practice to whittle and carve household utensils—bowls plates, spoons and such-like amenities. Probably, too, the more adept of the villagers would add carven decorations to their products.

Eventually, some of them would carve more than they could use themselves and sell what they had to spare to whoever would buy, during the summer months. And as the more skilled would demonstrate their ability to sell their wares more readily than the others, so would the ambitious strive to improve their technique.

By the fourteenth century, when the monastery at Ettal had become established, the call for souvenirs began to be met by carvings of religious figures; and, encouraged by the ever-rising demand, the craftsmen experimented and improved their skills until the passing merchants began to buy them in wholesale quantities, to carry with them to the wider markets beyond Bavaria. By the end of the fifteenth century the carven images from Oberammergau were famous in every major city in Europe—and woodcarving became the principal industry of the village. With their freedom from serfdom and their newfound wealth, the Oberammergauers began to listen to the tales told by the merchants of the wonders of Venice, of the Renaissance in Italy and to the descriptions of the arts and culture of Augsburg. Slowly, but with a gathering urge, the more ambitious citizens began to send their offspring out of the valley and beyond the Alps to see for themselves these new wonders—and to bring back with them a little of that culture and a measure of learning.

But the boom conditions in Oberammergau began to attract a great many undesirable hangers-on, and in the early sixteenth century the village became choked with army deserters from all nations, escaped prisoners, abandoned mercenaries—thieves, outcasts, fugitives and prostitutes. Almost before they were aware of what was happening, the villagers began to find that fear of these intruders by traders and merchants was beginning to scare them away—and causing a recession in business. So serious did the problem become, so overcrowded the houses, so prolific the petty thieving and so desperate the gangs of thugs that by the middle of the century the village councillors turned to the powerful Warden of Murnau for help.

The Warden gathered together the men from the long-established families of Oberammergau and led this strong and united force from door to door in the village. Every stranger, every uninvited lodger who had imposed himself on a householder, every outsider who had built himself a shelter, the beggars and the casual homeless were ousted and driven from the village. Those who refused to go of their own free will and those who returned were chained to carts and dragged across the border into Austria.

Politically, Oberammergau had only been vaguely

aware of the passing scene beyond the mountains during the fourteenth and fifteenth centuries. Deep in the mountains and content with their prosperity, they made no attempt to keep pace with the changing monarchy. In any event it would have proved a difficult task. For 200 years the succession had followed no set pattern; too often, as one duke died Bavaria would be divided amongst his surviving sons. Later, one son would absorb the heritage of another—and yet another generation of sons would re-divide what territories had not already been seized by various uncles—until but few in Bavaria knew, or cared, who was their titular head.

It was not until 1505 that Bavaria was re-united under a single monarch. In that year Albert the Wise came to power and in the following year tried to regularize the succession by decreeing that the duchy would pass, undivided in future, to the eldest son.

But the balmy days in Oberammergau were numbered. William IV succeeded Albert, and once more Bavaria was divided. In 1546 Martin Luther, the reformer, died, leaving behind in Germany a religious hiatus that carried with it lawlessness, destruction and chaos. Religious riots resulted in many of the principal cities of Germany being utterly burned. Mercenaries, who lived by the sword, anybody's sword, and were the friends of none, became pitiless in taking anything they wanted and could carry—and life became cheap.

In 1552 the Elector of Saxony captured Augsburg and in the same year struck south into the Ammer Valley. Ettal was plundered, two of the monks murdered, and the rest driven out—and for the first time the people of Oberammergau were seriously threatened by the Protestant forces of the Reformation.

In the turmoil the merchants refused to risk their lives and possessions on the roads of Germany and the flow of trade and pilgrims through the Ammer Valley ceased. Two hundred years of prosperity in Oberammergau had come to an end.

The seventeenth century opened in a welter of religious arguments and political threats. Millions of words were spoken, and hundreds of thousands written, in support of one religion and decrying all others. As many took an entirely different view—and yet more were used to decry both of them. The first decade of that century was the era of the tub-thumper and the pamphleteer—though the written word was still meaningless to the vast majority of the people and the verbal exhortations little understood by them. All that was achieved by them was strife, misunderstanding and political turmoil—and the German kings and princes began to align themselves with the religious creeds that, more often than not, gave them the best chance of preserving their thrones rather than salving their consciences.

The southern states of Germany soon returned to Catholicism, but the northern cities became more and more bigoted in the cause of the Reformation—and war became inevitable.

In 1618 Ferdinand II, the Catholic King of Bohemia, was dethroned by his subjects, who elected the Protestant Frederick in his place—and so occurred the first incident in what was to become the Thirty Years War.

Primarily, it was a religious war, in the early years confined to the German states, though, later, political affiliations added confusion to the issue. Like all religious wars, it bore with it all the horrors of fratricidal conflict, pointless destruction, looting, rape and wholesale murder. But, sheltered by the Alps, Oberammergau managed to remain aloof from the struggle. Indeed, it is believed that no single inhabitant of the village ever took any part in the long war.

But Oberammergau was not to escape the dire consequences of the rampaging armies as they drove backwards and forwards across the continent.

In April 1632 the Swede, Gustavus Adolphus, brought his highly professional and all-conquering army south to capture both Augsburg and Landsberg. He followed this up by forcing a passage across the River Lech and invading Bavaria.

A few days later he occupied Munich.

3 The Black Death and the Vow

The true source of the plague that struck southern Germany
in 1632 before rolling northwards over the European
continent, is not now known with any certainty.
Earlier outbreaks had almost invariably emanated from
the centuries-old breeding grounds of Egypt and Libya.
Contracted by traders and the crews of their ships, the
disease was then carried across the Mediterranean and into
the Italian ports—chief of which was Venice. Time after
time that watery city was decimated by the plague, but,
as often, its treasures and the volume of business that flowed
through it would attract fresh immigrants—either innocent of the danger or too greedy to care.

From there, the traders, bound for the inland cities,
would carry the germs with them into Austria and Germany, and then they would be spread even further afield
by the restlessly moving armies.

Some historians point to that dark continent south of the
Mediterranean as the starting point for the outbreak of
1632, but others assign the cause to the Thirty Years War
that had broken out in 1618.

Great areas of Germany had been ravaged by the con-
tending forces, cities had been burned, and, in many cases,

part of the population put to the sword. Each battle was fought with ruthless ferocity and with no regard for either life nor property. Surrender was pointless; the loser would be dispossessed of everything he owned—and probably slain as a useless encumbrance thereafter.

In terror whole populations would flee before an invading army, leaving behind the sick and the dead. Mercenaries, generally unpaid by their temporary masters, would loot the cities and warehouses, wreck the buildings and destroy the crops in an orgy of drunken mischief, torturing, raping and killing—before leaving the devastated area in search of sustenance and food again.

The injured, the sick and diseased, the dying and the helplessly aged were abandoned to fend for themselves—and the dead to rot in their beds or in the streets and back alleys. The most rudimentary sanitary systems broke down, cattle that had been slaughtered were too often thrown into the rivers and wells, and the filth of the cities added to the pollution. Garbage was left to decay in the streets and the vermin to race unchecked through the stinking, fly-infested dung-heaps.

Hunger, fear and the total destruction of their homes sent great tides of fleeing peoples washing over Europe. Some trekking north, others to the south; one wave of refugees would come up against another trudging in the opposite direction, turn aside—and find itself in an area already depopulated, burned and looted of supplies. Yet another crowd of destitute citizens would latch on to one or other of the armies—any army—in the hope of food and protection, only to be cut down in battle or cast aside into the barren lands of Europe to starve. Occasionally some desperate party would seek safety in the mountains—and die there through lack of food and shelter, too weak and exhausted to bury their dead and leaving a trail of rotting corpses to foul the streams and to mark their passing.

Yet for months Oberammergau remained free of the plague that resulted from this pestiferous charnel house. Remote, forgotten, since the flow of pilgrims to Ettal had ceased half a century earlier, difficult to approach across the forbidding Alps, through the deep snowbound passes and the dense forests, few of the miserable refugees had the strength left to face so daunting a journey.

Nor did the citizens of Oberammergau venture far from their valley. Knowing of the desperate situation on the far side of the mountain ranges, they would have been too fearful of the invading armies, of the powerful bands of outlaws and the merciless attacks of the disease-ridden, starving wretches from the ravaged cities to the north, to face the hazard. And so their isolation was preserved while the tide of pestilence continued to harass and create havoc in the centres of population beyond their Alpine fastness.

Despite the paucity of their communications, the people of Oberammergau must have known the precise details of the devastation being caused by the Black Death in the immediate vicinity, of the mass hysteria and of the terrible danger in which they stood. They would have learned that Garmisch-Partenkirchen to the east had suffered dreadfully, that Böbling had been utterly depopulated, and that in Kohlgrub only two couples remained alive to tell the tale of the terrible disaster that had struck their village.

In the old plague burial ground at Kohlgrub, there still stands a tiny church dedicated to St. Rochus, bearing an inscription to the effect that in gratitude for being delivered from the plague, the villagers would restore their church every hundredth year.

Gratitude! And only four poor souls surviving the holocaust to make such a pledge!

The citizens of Oberammergau, in those days, were probably more knowledgeable than the inhabitants of most of the villages outside the Ammer Valley. During the 200 years of their prosperity between 1350 and 1550, many of them had travelled far and wide and brought back with them an unusual learning. And, having been free of serfdom during all those years and having had the right to organize their own affairs, they had developed a self-sufficiency and the ability to administer their own community without outside help or direction.

In their wisdom therefore, and in the face of the approaching black pestilence, they began to institute precautions designed to ward it off. A ban was placed on all visitors to the village, and even their own people had to account in detail for any movement beyond the immediate neighbourhood. Journeys to other centres of population were forbidden, and only those employed in the local forests were permitted to return to their homes each night.

The housewives, as determined as their menfolk, enforced absolute cleanliness on their families and in their homes. Rats and other vermin were rooted out with ruthless persistence, furniture and floors were scoured, clothes, linen and bedding were scrubbed and bodies regularly bathed. At the same time, the elders of the village saw to it that all refuse was burned without any delay, that the wells were carefully guarded against being used as dumping places for rubbish and that the river was kept clear of the jetsam cast into it by the inhabitants of distant, upstream villages.

The sick were isolated until such time as they showed themselves to be uninfested by bubonic plague—and the number of services in the village church were increased to meet the growing demand for God's protection.

Then, in mid-summer the news reached the valley that Eschenlohe, a tiny hamlet not three miles from Oberammergau, had been overwhelmed by the Black Death. Within a matter of days, not a single house in the tiny mountain resort was left free from the plague, and before another ten days passed two thirds of the population had died.

Within an hour of the news reaching Oberammergau, the village elders—the Council of Six and Twelve, as it was called—met to discuss this latest threat to their own safety. Orders were issued to redouble the precautions that were already being taken, and additional rules were made with the object of strengthening the defences. All work in the village came to a standstill as even more guards were posted at each entrance, to check the flow of people, into and out of the tiny community. Axes, swords, cudgels, clubs and every other sort of weapon was issued to them so that they could enforce the ban on both refugees and casual wanderers; great bonfires were kindled on every access road, with the dual purpose of providing light so that the guards could see to it at night that no one approached the village unchallenged—and of burning up any airborne germs that might escape from the diseased bodies of those who were turned away.

Then, one final safeguard was clamped down on the little township. No one was to be allowed in or out of the village under any pretext whatsoever. And this ban was made effective from the moment it was issued—with no regard for the few unfortunate workers who were already outside the ring of sentries and not due to return until later in the day.

Kaspar Schisler, a day labourer who travelled regularly to and from his work near Eschenlohe, was one of these unlucky individuals. When he approached the village boundary that evening, returning to his wife and family, he found that his way was barred. No pleas were accepted by the guards; the fact that his home and his family were in the village and that he was a native of Oberammergau himself, were ignored—and Schisler was forced to return to the mountains.

These new, strict precautions were effective. For months the Black Death was kept out of Oberammergau. But inevitably, despite the ruthless determination of the villagers, human nature being what it was and still is, someone, sometime, was going to breach the defences— and unhappily, it was the '*Kirchweih*', the anniversary of the consecration of the village church that provided the sorry occasion.

It was in the autumn that this all-important festival in the calendar of most German communities was celebrated, though in the year 1632 but few towns or villages could have either the time, the opportunity or the heart to rejoice. In fact, Oberammergau was probably one of the very few places that had not either been wholly destroyed by one invading army or another or decimated by the plague and depopulated by the panic exodus of the survivors.

Still an unbroken, unravaged community, the people of Oberammergau prepared for the celebration. Though food was scarce, the women did their best to provide a feast and the men to decorate their homes and the village streets. They tried to ignore the fact that distant relatives and friends would not be allowed to join them during the three days of festivities, that the itinerant entertainers, showground people and the travelling children's side-show actors would be banned from setting up the usual fair, and that there would be no games or processions outside the village boundaries. Despite all this, they determined to dress up for the occasion, to attend Mass in the mornings as usual and to dance through most of each night.

And only three miles away, in some lonely hideout in the mountains, Kaspar Schisler must have sat, homesick and utterly depressed by the unhappy prohibition that kept him away from his home during those festive days. Would his wife be as unhappy as he was? Would his children miss him? Who could know the depths of his misery?

Probably, with no thought of endangering his family or any of the villagers, Schisler pondered deeply over the chances of creeping into the village and to his home unseen, of spending at the least a few hours in happy seclusion with his family—and then returning to his place in the mountains without anyone knowing of his visit to Oberammergau. Nor is it beyond the realms of speculation that he knew himself to have become infected by the plague and, in the mental horror and distress that followed, have lost all sense of reason and been drawn towards the only sympathetic haven that remained to him. And being a native of Oberammergau, Schisler would have known every back entry, every side lane and every unfrequented alley that led into the heart of the village.

Whatever it was that broke Schisler's endurance and over-bore his common sense, he came down from the mountains and after dark made his way along some little-known path until he reached his home. Village doors were not locked in those days and he would have slipped inside on the instant—and fallen into the arms of his long neglected family.

But there was to be no secret celebration for either him or his family. Almost before the greetings were over he complained of tiredness and lay down on the bed—yet his journey had been a short, familiar one. Nor could he be tempted by whatever food his wife had prepared for the *Kirchweith*.

By morning Schisler was feverish. His wife must have guessed at the danger, even before the symptoms made it obvious that he had been stricken by the plague. She must have suffered an agony of indecision over the need to inform the authorities of the dreadful incursion. Whether or not she reported the diseased condition of her husband at once, we do not know, but by the third day there could have been no further delay. Kaspar Schisler was dead of the plague.

Schisler was buried in all haste that same day, and his family isolated at once. But it was too late. His wife was the next to contract the horrible disease, followed within a matter of hours by each of their children. Before they died, one after the other, close friends began to show symptoms of having been infected—and there could be no further doubt that, at last, the Black Death had come to Oberammergau.

Desperately, the villagers fought to stem the tide of disaster. As each of its victims died, they were buried, almost before their bodies had chilled, in a deep pit that had been dug for the purpose, just beyond the confines of the village. Stricken houses were nailed up and the inmates condemned to fend for themselves until such time as they succumbed—or, in very rare cases, survived. But the battle had been lost from the moment Schisler had entered the village, and during the winter that followed the names of eighty-four men and women were recorded in the parish register of deaths, as having died of the plague.

But the register tells only part of the miserable tale. Primus Christeiner, the parish priest in 1632 whose duties included the maintenance of the registers—himself fell victim to the plague, and some time elapsed before his successor, Marcellus Fatiga, took up the dolorous task again—until he too died in the same way.

Great gaps appear in the register of deaths for the years 1632 and 1633, and the toll of the dead must have exceeded that shown in the written record. Nor were the names of children ever entered in the parish register of deaths.

Strangely too, Kaspar Schisler's name does not appear in that register—though it is recorded, together with those of his wife and children, in the *Oberammergau Memorial Book of the Year of the Plague.*

By the early summer of 1633 the villagers had long abandoned all hope of checking the epidemic through their own efforts, and it was then that the village elders—the elected Council of Six and Twelve, as it was called—turned their thoughts to God. Could this dreadful visitation be the consequence of the bitter religious wars that were ravaging Europe, and all the terrible happenings that went with it? Could it be the judgement of God?

The parish priest, a member of the council, said yes.

Days of discussion, even of argument, must have followed, but early in July the decision was made. On the chosen day the council led the survivors of the epidemic to the parish church. No one was excluded from the service. The sick and those already bedevilled by the plague were released from their isolation and helped on their way to the church. And, tiny though it was, there was more than enough room for all that was left of the community.

Led in prayer by the parish priest, supported by the Council of Six and Twelve and echoed by every member of the congregation, a solemn vow was made to God that they and their descendants would enact every tenth year, for ever, a Passion Play recalling the Last Supper, the Lord's arrest in the Garden of Gethsemane, His final condemnation by Pilate, His journey with the Cross to Calvary, His Crucifixion and the Resurrection—in return for His intercession and the passing of the Black Death from their midst.

And though the pestilence continued to take its merciless toll over all the lands beyond the Ammer Valley—even as far as Britain itself—not another soul died in Oberammergau of the plague.

4 Honouring the Vow

The vow made in 1633, pledging the villagers of Oberammergau to enact a Passion Play every tenth year, in perpetuity, was honoured for the first time less than a year later, in 1634.

No doubt it was a trivial affair in comparison with the gigantic production of today; the population was tiny and the mass graves held probably half of those who had inhabited the village a year earlier. Yet after the crushing terror of the plague and the almost unbelievable relief of the aftermath, it was most assuredly as heartfelt and devout a performance as was ever again to be given—even in the magnificent revivals of 300 years later.

Despite popular belief, the text used in the early Oberammergau Passion Plays was not an original script. It was an almost exact copy of the Augsburg Passion Play written by the monks of the Convent of St. Ulrich and St. Afra, as revised by Sebastian Wild nearly a century earlier.

Though the play was narrow in concept, contained no form of music, required no stage nor professional actors, its organization and eventual production could not have been accomplished with ease in those troublesome times. The disastrous Thirty Years War still continued and was to last for another fourteen years, with its plundering armies 'living off the land', deserters of many nations robbing and killing, and unpaid mobs of abandoned mercenaries raping and looting—and starving.

But it seemed to the citizens of Oberammergau that their village was too small and too isolated to be troubled seriously, and, slowly but surely, they began to put aside the unhappy memories of broken families, the stark appearance of the empty houses and the fear of invasion— and concentrated on making good their vow at the earliest possible date.

In dread that their promise, if neglected, might result in a resurgence of the plague? Who knows? Who can blame them if it was so?

Unfortunately we have no details of those of the villagers who took part in that initial production, but it seems certain that among today's cast quite a few of the actors are the direct descendants of, and still bear the names of, some of those who took part in that original 1634 play. And with this performance the cycle of Passion Plays was established as taking place in the fourth year of each of the following decades.

But before the second season opened in 1644, Oberammergau was plundered by a succession of armies as Bavaria became one of the principal battlegrounds of the long drawn out Thirty Years War. Trade became impossible, crops were destroyed, property was requisitioned, damaged beyond repair or burned, the women ravished, and those of the menfolk who were too slow to take to the mountains and forests in the face of each fresh onslaught, were brutally treated—and often murdered.

Yet in 1644 the Passion Play was produced for the second time—though history tells us almost nothing of the

faith that must have been needed to overcome the tremendous difficulties and hazards—the casting, the rehearsals
and the final production—never knowing what fate was
about to overtake them and their village.

The Thirty Years War came to an end in 1648 with the
Treaty of Westphalia. But Europe lay almost devastated.
Hoardes of people were left homeless, penniless and,
because the land had been neglected for years, starving.
Great armies of mercenaries found themselves stranded
far from their homes—also starving. The cessation of
hostilities, however, brought a faint gleam of hope to
Oberammergau, and in 1654, heedless of the still restlessly
moving refugees that flowed through the Ammer Valley,
they staged their Passion Play for the third time.

By 1664 conditions in Bavaria had improved substantially. Trade was beginning to move again over the great
routes, crops were being harvested, and the decades of
sullen fear and despair were slowly receding into the limbo
of history. Hope, still hardly believable, was beginning to
encourage industry—though almost a century was to go
by before the utter devastation of the first half of the
seventeenth century was to be wholly swept away.

In this upsurge of confidence, the fourth season of the
plays was undertaken with a new enthusiasm—and an
unexpected interest from visitors from beyond the valley.
Indeed, this tide of interest blossomed so much that the
Committee of the Play decided that the village church
was no longer big enough to accommodate the numbers to
be expected for the 1674 season. The venue was transferred, in consequence, to the churchyard—overlooking,
pathetically, the pits in which the victims of the plague
had been so hurriedly cast, forty years previously.

1674 was to be the last in the established cycle of the
fourth year in every decade as Passion Year. No record
exists of any reason for the change, but at some subsequent

date, the decision was made to hold the next Season of Plays in 1680—and every tenth year thereafter. This new cycle has persisted ever since, with only occasional variations caused by wars and interdicts.

2

Passion Play seasons followed one another in each of the next eight decades, and, because of a steadily developing technique and an equally virile improvement in the production, interest in the performance grew and spread beyond the Ammer Valley. In fact, so successful were the Oberammergau Passion Plays that imitations began to appear all over Bavaria—and into the northern cities of Germany.

Unfortunately, too many of these imitations were designed either as money-makers or with the intention of establishing reputations for ambitious writers. Plots became less and less worthy of the original concept of the Passion Play, others proved to be barely credible versions of the stories from the Bible—and some were no better than blood and thunder thrillers or out and out devil-rousers.

At the same time, by the middle of the eighteenth century, the peoples of Europe had emerged from the grinding poverty of the aftermath of the Thirty Years War. They had found a new, unaccustomed prosperity and, perhaps, in relief after the years of misery, could not resist taking full advantage of their new affluence in almost continuous celebrations, festivals and every other sort of mass entertainment. Theatres boomed, wine shops and ale-houses were crowded nightly with roisterers, all-night parties helped to disturb the peace of the few sleepers, and the squares were filled with music and dancing that lasted into the small hours. And as was to be expected, abuses and excesses rode on the tide of unlimited pleasure. Bavaria in the past had always maintained a deep sense of religion—and the good behaviour that went with it. Bavarians had been only barely diverted from Catholicism by the Reformation and had returned with heartfelt relief to the teachings of Rome within a very few years, leaving the new religions to take permanent root in the north of Germany and the Low Countries. But very many thousands of refugees had settled in the Electorate after the war, and it was chiefly among their descendents that this wave of unbridled, uninhibited freedom ran amok.

Maximilian Joseph ascended the throne of Bavaria in 1745, frowning heavily on the rising neglect of the church by his people. He despised them for the blasphemous way they parodied religious practices, for the way in which they debased religious festivals and for their total disregard for the teachings of the church. But neither his expressed displeasure or the dark hints put out by the members of his government served to check the libertines.

In March 1770, losing all patience with his people, the Elector decided that an end must be put to these excesses. In an attempt to bridle the blasphemous, pseudo-religious exhibitions that had mushroomed in his kingdom, he issued an edict prohibiting the performance of all religious plays—which, of course, included Passion Plays. He hoped by this means to put a term to all other religious excesses and eventually to restore his people to a more decorous way of life.

Oberammergau had been wholly free of such irreligious practices, and its citizens were deeply shocked by the unexpected ban. Apart from the fact that the Season of Plays had become a major event in the valley, its fame had spread until visitors were to be expected from Munich and even further afield. Besides, preparations for the 1770

Season were complete, and the players proficient in their parts.

But of much greater importance to the villagers was the fact that the prohibition meant that they were forced into breaking the solemn vow that had been made on their behalf, by their forebears, long ago.

The Council of Six and Twelve appealed at once to the Ecclesiastical Courts for relief, producing the text of their play as evidence of the sincerity of its story, recalling the rights bestowed on them to conduct their own affairs by Ludwig the Bavarian as far back as 1332—and quoting the details of the vow made at the time of the plague in 1633.

But in Munich the council received only a cold refusal to exempt Oberammergau from the edict.

Though we have no record of what further steps were taken to evade the prohibition, two points lead us to believe that the people of Oberammergau decided to ignore the order, in the hope of being out of reach of reprisals in the remote fastness of their valley. There are records in the parish accounts that show expenditure on the Passion Play that year, and there is shown too, that an admission charge was made—for the first time.

No doubt this levy on visitors had become necessary because of the broadening scale of the production and the loss of wages to many of the actors because of the growing number of performances required to satisfy the demand.

Charles Theodore succeeded Maximilian Joseph in 1777, and though the edict prohibiting religious exhibitions and plays remained part of the law, it was less strictly enforced and the citizens of Oberammergau went ahead with their preparations for the 1780 season with some confidence. Nevertheless, just in case some officious member of the government should suddenly decide to reinforce the ban, the Council of Six and Twelve appealed to the Elector to lift the prohibition from their community.

To the immense gratification of the villagers of Oberammergau, Charles Theodore, after considering the application and taking advice concerning the text, gave his assent to the opening of that season—and to the series being continued every tenth year thereafter.

The Passion Play Year of 1790 passed without let or hindrance, but in 1791 the Elector was persuaded to renew the edict—making no exceptions.

In 1795 the French invaded Bavaria, and in the following year Charles Theodore fled. He was succeeded by Maximilian II in 1799, soon after the Austrians reoccupied Bavaria. He promptly set about revising the laws in a more liberal manner, giving the people more say in the administration of their towns and cities—but he suppressed all religious houses.

3

The Council of Oberammergau, despite the continued ban on religious performances, the new oppressive laws against religious houses and the occupation of their country by the Austrians, still felt some measure of security from government interference in the inaccessible stronghold of their valley, and, with the stout courage of a positive faith, went ahead with their preparations for the 1800 Season of Passion Plays.

But they were soon to learn that the Ammer Valley was no longer a Shangri-la. They gave three performances in May of that year, but in June the village was occupied by Austrian troops. Two more performances were given, attended by many of the Austrians, but the season came to an abrupt end on 12th July when a battle was fought between the Austrians and the French in the Ammer

Valley—and Oberammergau came under bombardment. Fortunately the damage was slight, though the house of the Parish Priest was set ablaze. The French were driven off with difficulty and the Austrians were left so much on the defensive, that it was not possible to revive the interrupted season.

In December 1800 the Austrians were finally driven out by the French, and in 1801 the villagers were given permission to stage a further four performances of the play, in the hope that they might be able to recover at least some part of the financial loss they had suffered in the previous year. The plays were in fact given, but, in the uncertainty of the times, probably added to rather than reduced the debt incurred.

By 1810, the year in which the twentieth season of Passion Plays was due to be held, it seemed virtually certain that the vow made by the survivors of the plague, was to be broken. Count Monteglas had risen to power as Chief Minister to Maximilian II, and he made it clear that Passion Plays and similar religious exhibitions, were not to be revived.

The Council of Six and Twelve were not prepared to accept the count's ruling, and, under the leadership of the courageous Georg Lang, they made their way to Munich. There they did everything possible to obtain a reversal of the ruling banning their play, but Count Monteglas, deeply influenced by the French under the meteoric Napoleon Bonaparte, whose policies included the secularization of the monasteries and a stern-eyed view of any religious exercises that tended to lessen his own image, was adamant.

Georg Lang, still unwilling to concede defeat, sought the help of an old friend of his, the ex-tutor to the Crown Prince. Georg Anton Sambuya, being a native of Oberammergau, was deeply sympathetic and succeeded in persuading the Elector to give audience to the deputation.

Georg Lang and the council must have been most persuasive as the King overruled his Chief Minister and authorized the performance of the Oberammergau Passion Plays.

However, by then, it was too late to produce the play that year, but preparations went ahead at once to hold the season in 1811.

Fortune was not to be with the producers of the play in that year, however. Napoleon was rampaging all over Europe at the time, and frontiers were changing almost day by day. People stayed at home—unless they were dragooned into one army or another. Indeed, a number of men from Oberammergau—nine of whom died fought with the French army. Taxes were penal in order that armies could be supplied, farms were left short of labour, food was scarce and travel conditions dangerous. In the face of these adverse conditions only six performances of the Passion Play were staged in 1811.

But Napoleon's star faded even faster than it had prospered, and in April 1814 he was forced to abdicate, leaving behind a debt-ridden Europe and mass unemployment, as the great armies fell apart and dispersed.

Eleven performances of the Passion Play were given in 1815 in the declared hope of making some provision for the local unemployed, but it was not a success. The hoped-for visitors remained at home, financially exhausted and still fearful of the future. In fact, the season almost came to an end before it opened; Napoleon escaped from Elba and landed in France on 1st March, and it was not until after his defeat at Waterloo on 18th June that panic died down again.

The unfortunate season of 1815 was followed by even more tragic times for the people of Oberammergau. In 1816 the harvest failed, and the villagers were quickly reduced to starvation level. To add to their distress, in

November 1817, just as they were recovering in some measure from the previous year's famine, a disastrous fire destroyed a large portion of the village. The homeless had to endure a bitter winter huddled in already over-crowded houses or in makeshift shelters built from what-ever could be salvaged from the ruins.

After the hunger and misery of those years, a slow recovery followed. By the middle of 1819 the community had regained sufficient heart to set about planning and preparing for 1820, the next in the proper cycle of seasons in which the Passion Play should be staged.

To their surprise, the demand for seats far exceeded those available. Indeed, so great was the interest that before the next season approached, the Committee of the Play decided that the old village churchyard, wherein the victims of the plague had been buried almost 200 years earlier, was no longer large enough to accommodate the number of visitors to be expected.

After months of discussions, many suggestions and the inspection of a number of possible venues, the site chosen for the 1830 season by the Committee of the Play and the Council of Six and Twelve, was a large meadow just beyond the confines of the village. It became known as the 'Passion Meadow'—and on it today stands the vast Passion Theatre.

A larger, better-equipped stage was erected on this new site and, perhaps because of the broadening scope of the play and the much larger audiences, it began to snowball on itself.

By 1840 visitors began to arrive from far beyond the frontiers of Bavaria. The Crown Prince Maximilian, too, helped to build a widening enthusiasm by setting up a country house for himself near Hohenschwangau, close to the Austrian border and only about fifteen miles from Oberammergau. Eventually he rebuilt Hohenschwangau

Castle as a summer residence for the Royal Family—bringing very many important and influential visitors to the region.

Eduard Devrient, the famous actor and historian, saw one of the plays during the 1850 season, and his articles on the subject were published internationally, expanding the interest in the story of Oberammergau and the number of visitors who determined to see one of the productions.

Many of the élite of Europe visited Oberammergau during the season of 1860, though the valley was still difficult of access over a mountainous, unmetalled road that made the journey a penance to all but the true enthusiasts.

By 1870 a railway line ran to Weilheim from Munich and the play committee, anticipating an even greater flow of visitors than ever, arranged to stage a record number of performances—some twenty in all. But, unfortunately, once again a Passion Play Season was interrupted by war. Sixteen performances only were given before the outbreak of the Franco-Prussian War put an end to the season.

In 1870 even Joseph Mayr, the Christ of the Play, was called up for service with the army, but, as the fighting was far from the Ammer Valley, he was employed, purely on garrison duties, so that there should be no need for him to shave off his beard.

Within a matter of months, the French were overwhelmed, and on 28th January 1871 they sued for an armistice.

In a rush of enthusiasm, the abandoned Passion Play Season was resumed in that year, and so great was the demand for tickets that nineteen performances were staged.

In that year too, the Prince of Wales (later King Edward VII) and Princess Alexandra saw one of the performances, travelling to Oberammergau incognito as the Baron and Baroness Renfrew.

By 1880 the railway from Munich had been extended to Murnau, only fifteen miles from Oberammergau and to Garmisch-Partenkirchen in time for the 1890 season.

4

The 1900 season saw the railway line from Munich extended all the way to Oberammergau, and electrified. What had been a two-day journey over difficult roads and mountain passes thirty years earlier, became a comfortable, smooth, high-speed journey that took little more than two hours to complete. In consequence, no fewer than forty-eight performances were needed to accommodate all those who wanted to see the Passion Play.

By 1910 the demand for seats to see one or other of the performances came in from all over the world. Fifty-six times the play had to be staged between May and September of that year and as many as 5,000 tickets were sold for each performance.

But once again war disrupted the regular cycle of Oberammergau Passion Seasons. In 1914 the First World War cast its ugly shadow across the face of Europe, and by the time it ended in 1918 eight and a half million people had died in the conflict. The German Empire ceased to exist, their people reduced to absolute poverty and on the verge of revolution—and even the victorious nations to the verge of bankruptcy.

There could be no possible hope of meeting the 1920 date for the next season of Passion Plays. Political storms tore at the heart of Germany, demands for reparations by the Allies were impossible to meet, crops had been neglected and food was scarce—and faith in God had suffered a tremendous reverse.

But in 1922 the citizens of Oberammergau determinedly set to work to honour the vow that had been made nearly

290 years earlier. Unhappily, in that year the spiralling inflation in Germany suddenly broke all bounds and soared beyond control. Currency became worthless overnight; postage stamps that had sold for less than a mark before the war, rocketed to an unbelievable 10,000,000 marks. Token money was printed, even in denominations of 50,000,000 marks—and lost all value within a matter of hours.

Yet this new appalling disaster failed to overawe the Committee of the Passion Play, and, with immense courage and few resources, a record number of sixty-eight performances were given before a total audience of over 310,000.

Slowly, Germany began to recover from the financial debacle—until the New York Stock Market crashed in 1929, wrecking the American economy, tumbling the *bourses* of Europe and foreshadowing world-wide mass unemployment.

Yet again, despite the new depression, the people of Oberammergau set about preparing for the thirty-second season of plays due to be produced in 1930. And wholly unexpectedly in those workless days, eighty performances were given to a total of 380,000 visitors.

Quickly the economic crisis in Germany reached the same chaotic proportions as occurred less than a decade earlier. Mass unemployment, hunger and abject misery followed, and in desperation the people began to listen to any frenzied rabble-rouser who promised them hope—and the destruction of those who were said to have caused the depression. Adolf Hitler and his National Socialist Party claimed their attention.

At the peak of the depression in 1932, an American film company offered the people of Oberammergau a million dollars for the right to make a film version of the Passion Play. But even in those poverty-stricken days,

(*above*) The Church of St. Peter and St. Paul, first setting for the play

(*below*) The Play in progress in 1870

The Passion Play Theatre; (*left*) looking towards the auditorium from the stage end

(*above*) The crowning with thorns (Act XII)

(*below*) The crucifixion (Act XV)

The descent from the Cross (Act XV)

(*above*) The Resurrection (Act XVI)

(*below*) The Ascension (Tableau to Finale)

(*above*) Expulsion of Adam and Eve from Paradise (Tableau to Prelude)

(*below*) Tobias leaves his parents (Tableau to Act III)

Characters in the 1960 play: (a) Peter – Hans Mayr Sr.; (b) Pilate – Melchior Breitsamter Jr.; (c) Caiaphas – Benedikt Stückl; (d) Herod – Arthur Maser

Anton Lang as Christ in 1910

when German money could buy little indeed, the villagers refused to commercialize what was to them a sacred trust.

In 1933, however, money was desperately needed to meet the commitments entered into for the benefit of the community before the financial collapse of Germany. Though immense sums had been garnered through the box offices during the Passion Play Seasons of both 1922 and 1930, the depression that succeeded each of them had reduced its purchase power to almost nil.

Because of the urgent need for funds, the Americans were permitted to sponsor the visit of certain of the leading Passion Play actors, on a goodwill tour of the United States. As it turned out, the visit became a high-powered sales drive, and so successful was it that the Committee of the Play determined to attempt what had long been at the back of their minds—a season of Passion Plays in 1934, to celebrate the tercentenary of the vow and the passing of the plague.

The thirty-third season proved to be a tremendous success, and more than 400,000 visitors saw one or other of the eighty-four performances—but, already the shadow of events was beginning to darken the future.

In June 1934 there occurred the Nazi Blood Purge—centred around Bad Wiessee and Munich—which destroyed all opposition to Hitler. In August, the aging Hindenburg died, leaving Hitler as the sole authority in the Reich. Once again war was to interrupt the regular cycle of Passion Plays—this time leaving a gap in the series that was never to be filled.

In August 1939, Hitler ordered the invasion of Poland, and a few days later Britain and France went to her assistance. In consequence, the election for the parts in the Oberammergau Passion Play, usually held in the September preceding each season, had to be abandoned. In 1940, on the very day that the season should have opened,

4

the defeated British Army was being evacuated from the Continent through Dunkirk.

Oberammergau sank back into the past; a remote, unimportant, forgotten village, deep in the recesses of the Bavarian Alps. Once or twice the German armaments authorities considered the possibility of establishing secret weapons factories in the Ammer Valley, but a tactful burgomaster succeeded in discouraging them. Except for the steady departure of those called up for service in the armed forces of the Reich and the inevitable shortages created by war, Oberammergau was to remain a sheltered haven, untouched by the shattering air raids that were crumbling the cities of Europe.

Not until 1944, when as S.S. headquarters was set up in Linderhof Castle nearby, were there to be any military establishments in the valley to attract reprisals from the British and American Air Forces. But the S.S. built no defences, and, as a result, when the American troops penetrated the Ammergau Valley in 1945, there was no battle in or around Oberammergau and no destruction of property, or loss of life.

The war ended in May of that year, leaving Germany in abject defeat; its cities heaps of rubble and its survivors homeless and starving. Once again refugees trudged hopelessly across the nation in search of relatives, food and shelter—rarely succeeding in their quest.

Bavaria was occupied by the United States forces, and by 1947 they had built themselves large recreation centres in and around Oberammergau. In 1949 they began to take an interest in the history of the Passion Play and to urge the local population to revive the series. But hunger, unemployment, the loss of many Oberammergauers in the fighting, and yet again, the total collapse of the German monetary system, left little scope for any such undertaking.

The Americans persisted with their encouragement and helped the preparations with food, timber and much else that could not have been obtained without assistance, so that despite many doubts and difficulties, the Committee of the Passion Play was again elected by the community to organize the 1950 season.

Though food rationing was still severe and the factories had barely started to turn out the necessities of life again, the production proved to be a tremendous success. For the first time, over half a million visitors saw the Passion Play.

From that date forward, the economic conditions in Germany began to improve. Rebuilding and the resurgence of industry went ahead so rapidly, that the rest of the world looked on in astounded disbelief—and prosperity came to Oberammergau again.

By 1959 it seemed that the whole world was anxious to see the Passion Play, and for the first time in many decades, nothing stood in the way. So widespread was the demand for every trifle of news concerning the progress being made towards the 1960 season of Plays, that the Committee of the Play was inundated with requests to provide facilities for reporting the details of the election of actors to the various roles, due to take place some eight months before the Season was due to open.

Telephones, teleprinters, telex, radio and television transmission services were installed in time for the event, and as the results of the election were declared, they were chalked up on a board outside the theatre, where a vast crowd watched and waited. Within minutes, the names of those chosen for the many parts was known in every major city in the world. But in the crowd of Oberammergauers around the board, many a tear was held back with difficulty. Of joy—and of sad disappointment.

The 1960 season opened in May of that year, untrammelled by outside events, and, despite a theatre that now held 6,000 at every performance, not much more than half the demand for seats could be met.

In such boom conditions, ticket agents were negotiating for seats for the 1970 season of Passion Plays almost before the 1960 season had come to an end—and by 1967 tour organizers throughout the world had all their plans laid; accommodation in hotels, transport detailed and pamphlets and brochures printed and issued to the public. By 1968 bookings had reached unprecedented proportions.

Unhappily, however, the success of the 1970 season was threatened by the determination of a powerful American Jewish Christian group to boycott the Passion Play on the grounds that it was anti-semitic. It could not be forgotten that during the tercentenary performances of 1934, the burgeoning Nazi party in Germany used the Passion Play as propaganda in support of its own anti-Jewish policies.

The boycott was, in some degree, effective and encouraged the American group to harden its resolve to intensify its campaign. By 1977 the Council of Oberammergau decided that the time had come to take notice of the rising tide of opinion. It was then proposed that the present day version of the Passion Play should be replaced by the older, 1750 edition. The suggestion created wide dissension in the village—until it was realized that neither the present nor the older version would satisfy the demands of the critics.

A compromise was found just in time to go into rehearsal for the 1980 season. Every hint of anti-semitism was carefully deleted from the present day script. It achieved a major success—and the villagers then prepared themselves with confidence for the 350th anniversary of the first performance of the Passion Play, to be staged during 1984.

5 The Text and the Music

The early editions of the Passion Play contained no music, neither vocal nor instrumental; nor was the script originally written for the sole purpose of honouring the vow made by the people of Oberammergau in 1633. Passion Plays were, in fact, enacted in the village church many years earlier.

It seems probable that those earlier plays were sponsored by the monks of Ettal—indeed it was unlikely that anyone in the village, other than the village priest perhaps, had the skill to read or write.

Unfortunately no copy of any of those very early editions still exists; the oldest version, still treasured among the Oberammergau parish records, is dated 1662. It bears an endorsement that reads, "Has again been revised and rewritten . . . " and is an almost exact copy of the Augsburg Passion Play of St. Ulrich and St. Afra, first performed in that city somewhere around 1450, and a second similar play written by Sebastian Wild, a Mastersinger of Augsburg in the sixteenth century.

This text was retained by the Oberammergau Players for more than a hundred years, until an entirely new version was written by Father Ferdinand Rosner, Librarian and Keeper of the Muniments (furnishings and equipment) at the Ettal Monastery.

Rosner was known to be a brilliant dramatist and had written a number of plays—some of which are performed in Germany to this day. Because of his reputation his version of the Passion Play was accepted by the community and used for the first time in 1750.

Unfortunately the character of the new text proved to be too Italiante in concept and too full of condemnation in the 'hell and damnation' manner of many of the preachers of that era to be welcomed without criticism. It was difficult to follow, too. The players disliked it, the church authorities rejected it, and the public either misunderstood it or resented the unrelieved 'doom' it promised.

But in 1770 the Elector Maximilian Joseph issued an edict prohibiting the performance of all Passion Plays throughout Bavaria. He was driven to make this ban because of the fast growing tendency to satire and to deviate from the Bible story of the Passion, among the writers of that period.

Though the people of Oberammergau appear to have side-stepped the ban, it seemed to them wise to prepare a new text in the hope that it would be received more favourably by the Church authorities and by the newly created College of Censors that had been empanelled in Munich.

The Committee of the Play approached Father Magnus Knipfelberger, another of the Ettal Benedictine monks— who had at one time been a pupil of Rosner. He gladly undertook the task of writing a more acceptable script in time for the next season of plays.

As it turned out the improvements, if any, were chiefly concerned with cutting many of the 'hellfire' passages from Rosner's Play and transferring the 'sermons' to the chorus.

Evidently this new text gave the authorities less offence as it was brought into use in 1780, repeated in 1790 and again in the broken season of 1800–1801.

But it was never a success. The actors found it too 'foreign' and too 'unreal' to be played with sincerity and a proper understanding by such as they—labourers, small farmers and foresters—and audiences were unimpressed and inclined to be bored by the flowery dialogue. They craved something more substantial and a genuine portrayal of the solemnity of the Passion.

Ottmar Weis rewrote the whole of the text of the Oberammergau Passion Play in time for the season of 1810. He was educated in his early years at Ettal where he, in his turn received tuition from the writer Knipfelberger. After some advanced teaching in Munich he returned to the Monastery of Ettal where he was ordained priest in 1795 and sent as the parish priest to Eschenlohe.

In 1803 Ettal Monastery was dissolved by the secular authority, but Weis, shocked by the event, left his parish and returned to Ettal to live there entirely alone. Though he did a great deal of teaching in the village of Oberau and spent much of his spare time in caring for the monastery, Weis was able to do a good deal of writing.

In preparing his new version of the Passion Play, Ottmar Weis made a point of adhering to the Bible story, producing a straightforward, complete drama; but, because of the edict prohibiting such performances, he had to wait until 1811 before he saw it produced.

It was received at once with solemn approval by players and audience alike.

But Weis was by no means content with his work and rewrote the whole of the text in time for the twenty-first season of plays to be staged in 1815.

No doubt the dignity and pathos of Weis's play owed a

great deal to the music composed for it by Rochus Dedler. Dedler was a native of Oberammergau; his father an innkeeper in the village. He was educated first in the village school, where his teacher found him to be passionately interested in music. His parents then tried and succeeded in getting him accepted as a choir boy at Rottenbuch, and from there he progressed to the seminary at Munich. Dedler had hoped to become ordained as a priest but his purpose was defeated by the dissolution of the monasteries, ordered by the Elector Maximilian II in 1799.

Rochus Dedler was fortunate in being offered the vacant post of schoolteacher in Oberammergau, though he must have deeply regretted the need to accept it—but education in those days was a hindrance rather than an asset without either family or patronage to create a profitable opening.

Dedler proved himself to be a brilliant musician and an extremely talented composer, particularly in the field of sacred music, but unfortunately much of his work became scattered and received little attention during his lifetime. This despite his success in composing an operetta that was performed as part of the celebrations on the occasion of the state entry of the Elector Maximilian Joseph into the city of Munich.

Not until he composed the score for the Oberammergau Passion Play and had it performed there, was any attention paid to his music. Nor was any serious attempt made until years later to gather his works together. But the disastrous fire that destroyed more than half of Oberammergau in 1817 did much to frustrate the endeavour. The school, where he kept his papers, was one of the buildings gutted by the flames.

Rochus Dedler was not the first to compose a musical score for the Passion Plays of Oberammergau. Though the original scripts called for no music, vocal parts were introduced as time went by, until there was the need for a complete choir—known in due course as the 'Guardian Angels'. But no name stands out in this connection, and it is safe to assume that the music was inserted piecemeal, by those who had written or revised the text, since its inception more than 170 years ago.

Dedler's music for the Passion Play needed to be re-written twice. The original version used in the 1811 production had to be revised in line with the alterations made to the text by Weis, in time for the season of 1815, and then, unfortunately, this second composition was destroyed in the fire of 1817. His third score was ready in time for the opening of the Passion Season of 1820, when the plays were performed for the first time in the Passion Meadow.

Two years later Rochus Dedler died aged 44.

A year before his death, Dedler composed the music for and Weis preached the sermon at the Mass in honour of a newly ordained priest, Father Alois Daisenberger.

Alois Daisenberger was born in the village of Oberau and was at one time a pupil of Weis in Oberammergau—and with such a tutor and the play that absorbed so much of his attention, it was hardly cause for wonder that Daisenberger developed an abiding enthusiasm for the Passion Plays.

He had a distinct flair for writing drama and an unmistakable facility for scripting the passages in a text so that the ordinary, not very well educated person, could follow the plot without difficulty. In the atmosphere of Oberammergau he studied the Weis version of the Passion Play with deep interest, aware that times and fashions, moods and fervours, were changing. Then, with care and understanding he adapted, rather than rewrote the play, into a more up-to-date presentation.

Daisenberger's version was widely welcomed at its first performance in 1850—and continued to be used, with only minor modifications during the next hundred years.

Alois Daisenberger died in 1883 at the age of 84, venerated by the community whom he refused to leave during his long sojourn there, either for promotion or in his retirement.

The musical score by Rochus Dedler was treated with less respect as the years went by. Successive conductors had ideas of their own and were much inclined to impose them upon the original version, until the score became no better than a hotch-potch of widely differing interpretations. In 1949 the Committee of the Passion Play commissioned Eugene Pabst to rewrite the whole composition.

Pabst set about the task with enthusiasm. He cut away the tangled web of alterations that had crept in since Dedler's death more than 120 years ago and re-established that great musician's original score. But he did improve many of the phrases and passages—without diverting from the Dedler interpretation.

Pabst's work was introduced in time for the 1950 season and was widely acclaimed as a polished return to the earlier and more dignified conception of the musical score.

Much argument has gone on ever since, despite the high regard both the players and the public have for Pabst's version of the music for the Passion Play. Some critics are inclined to insist that a truly modern interpretation be given to the whole production, others claim that Dedler was inclined to the popular at the expense of the ritualistic and yet others decry the overlong choral arrangements. Unhappily, it is probable that another spate of alterations, revisions and interpolations will be imposed on the score during the present century and beyond, before some brilliant composer steps forward to produce an entirely new version.

An American Jewish Christian group brought into the open a longstanding complaint that the Passion Play was anti-semitic and called for a boycott of the 1970 season. Audiences dwindled embarrassingly. The Daisenberger version incorporated the words spoken in the gospels, but he had needed to add substantially to the dialogue to produce a full six hours' drama. It was chiefly to these additions that the critics objected.

Hans Schwaighofer, who had played the part of Judas during the two previous seasons and had, on occasions, deputized for Georg Lang as producer, was appointed Pageant Master and given the task of finding a solution to the dispute.

Unable to find a villager capable of producing an alternative script, Schwaighofer reintroduced the version written by Rosner as far back as 1750. In 1977 the village council advanced £125,000 to finance a full-scale try-out of the older text. It was declared to be a success. But during the 1978 elections, prior to the 1980 season, attitudes changed and the villagers began to take sides in what was to become a bitter dispute. The Daisenberger faction, with its support for the text that had been so successful during the past hundred years, carried the day against those who sought to revive the eighteenth-century archaic, allegorical style of Rosner.

Schwaighofer resigned.

Hurriedly, a pastor residing in the monastery at Ettal, set to work to delete, or amend, every passage in the Daisenberger text that could be construed in any way as denigrating the Jews.

It was a notable achievement and the 1980 audiences received the compromise version with almost fanatical approval.

6 Choosing the Cast

Despite the immense publicity and the furore of world-wide interest that is aroused by the approach of each Passion Season, the people of Oberammergau do nothing to relax the rules they have made for themselves, in a positive determination to ensure that the Passion Play is performed in the spirit in which the vow was made by their ancestors more than 300 years ago.

Though the scale of the production, the size of the cast, the enormous theatre and the vast crowds of visitors that have swelled beyond any possibility of belief by those who attended that desperate service in the village church back in 1633, the villagers of today have no wish to change the Passion Play from the devout fulfilment of that long ago vow, into a commercial drama nor into a pseudo-religious exhibition.

The tremendous publicity that has created so wide an interest, is not initially of their seeking—though in practice, the community of Oberammergau has taken advantage of the consequences of the free advertisements in the conduct of their private affairs. Hotels, boarding houses, restaurants, shops, souvenirs and all the concomitants of a tourist centre, have sprung up under the umbrella of the Passion

Plays, and individual profits have often been high.

But the plays are still staged only under the age old restrictions that keep it the private concern of the citizens of Oberammergau. Thousands, hundreds of thousands, witness the plays each season, but only the villagers may take part in honouring the old, solemn promise on the stage of the Passion Theatre.

In fact, only those who were born in Oberammergau, or those who have made the village their permanent home and resided there for not less than twenty years, are eligible to take any part in the play. And because of this simple rule there never has been, nor ever will be, any shortage of experienced performers among the local people. The children—even babies in arms—have their parts to play, and the eagerness of these tots to get walk-on parts, and their enthusiasm on the stage, creates an unending pool of potential principals as they progress from decade to decade.

Because of this reserve of practiced players and the fact that the play is an intensely personal affair, the committee have invariably refused all offers of help, whatever the qualifications or status of the donor, and whatever the fame of the actor or actress.

In no sense are the Oberammergau players professionals. Each and every one of them has his own occupation—and makes his living by it. Only during the actual performance is he permitted to leave his work—and immediately afterwards he must return to his trade or profession.

No individual publicity is permitted to any member of the cast—though it has been found impossible to keep the fame of some of the principal actors becoming renowned. No performances are permitted other than in Oberammergau, and no personal appearances are allowed.

Restrictions on reporters and photographers in the village cannot be enforced—though no cameras are allowed to be taken into the Passion Theatre during a performance. Press photographers make their appearance in force a year or more before the season commences, snapping any and everyone who might stand some chance of being cast in one or other of the principal roles and picking up background material from the parish registers. But no Oberammergauer will prosper from any such publicity.

Nor will the pressmen gain much information from the people of Oberammergau as to who amongst them are likely to be chosen for parts—but speculation cannot be altogether controlled.

No wigs, false beards or any form of make-up is permitted, and, in consequence, those who may hope to be given parts, must allow their hair and beards to grow unchecked and unstyled for a year before the Passion Play Season is due to open—adding spice to the inevitable speculation.

This rule is not merely a matter of tradition, but very necessary where the stage is open to the elements and the players must act their parts in all sorts of weather conditions, from rainstorms to burning sunshine—as nature dictates.

No married woman, nor any over the age of 35, may take part. Many a village maiden has postponed her wedding for as long as ten years in the hope of being given a role in the play, and many another, having once been selected, has compelled some unfortunate boy friend to wait yet another ten years, until after the next season of plays. Nor do these hopeful girls spend much time with their fiancés; they must take part in the series of practice plays that fill the inter-season years, if they hope to gain both experience and to catch the attention of committee members. Nor dare they risk the censure of gossiping tongues as only villagers of impeccable character are eligible for parts in the play. And even in Oberammergau, jealousy and intrigue are not entirely unknown. Maybe it is as well that there are few parts for women in the Passion Play.

Preparations for each Passion Season commences some years in advance. Indeed, negotiations for block seat bookings by ticket agencies, tour organizers and other professionally interested bodies, begins almost immediately after the last performance of the season, in readiness for the next—ten years ahead.

Two years in advance of the season a meeting of the villagers is convened by the burgomaster, when, in accordance with tradition, he relates the story of the vow made by their ancestors so many years ago. He then calls upon them to affirm that they are in favour of preparing, once again, for another season in the cycle of plays.

Later, the Committee of the Passion Play is elected, also in accordance with long established tradition. As always, the burgomaster is elected as chairman and the parish priest as his deputy. All sixteen members of the village council are chosen, *en bloc*, leaving only six places to be filled in a free vote—though every candidate is expected to have had considerable experience of the play in one form or another.

The twenty-four members of the committee choose the director for the season from their own number. They are then responsible for the organization of all facets of the forthcoming production and the supporting administration, including such items as the furbishing of the theatre, arrangements for transport, catering, bookings, rehearsals and casting.

Perhaps the most publicized of these is the allocation of the many parts to the players.

In the September preceding each season, the committee meets to elect some 1,200 players to the various roles that have to be performed—123 of them being speaking parts. About 200 children have to be included in the cast.

In making their choice, the members of the committee must take into account the ability of those under consideration to act their parts, the aptness of their appearance, their enthusiasm, freedom to give their whole attention to rehearsals and all of their time during the long summer season to the play, their moral characters, general demeanour and public reputation—a truly daunting task.

Election day opens with a Passion service in the parish church, attended by all the members of the play committee—and always there is a full and excited congregation present. The committee then adjourns to the foyer of the Passion Theatre, where, in the presence of a host of reporters, the burgomaster, as chairman of the committee, calls upon the members to promise to choose only actors who are entirely suitable for their parts. Immediately afterwards the foyer is left to the committee and its deliberations.

As the actors are chosen by secret ballot or, in the event of a tie, by the producer of the play, the names of the successful contenders are chalked up on a noticeboard in the square outside the theatre, before a tense and anxious throng of villagers. It is usual to allocate the speaking parts on the first day of the elections, taking the principal roles first.

At first sight it would seem that the committee had an almost impossible task in choosing such a vast cast, but in practice the members are generally aware of the ability and the reputation of each of the candidates; they live amongst them and see, year by year, the regular 'training plays' that take place between the seasons.

Rehearsals commence almost immediately the parts have been cast. As no payments are made to any of the performers until the season is over, rehearsals have to be arranged to fit in, as far as possible, with the players' normal occupations—a difficult and lengthy business, where so many people in such a variety of trades and professions is concerned, if hardship is to be avoided. In any event, those taking part can only look forward to token payments, limited to recompensing them for the hours actually spent on the stage during public performances, when it was clearly impossible for them to engage in their normal employment.

The duration of each performance, some seven hours, and the vast concourse of actors, lays a heavy burden on the director. It means too, that the actors must forgo almost every moment of their leisure hours if they are to become word-perfect while still earning their daily bread. Nor is that devotion limited to the mouths immediately preceding and during the Passion Play Season, for those who are ambitious and eager enough to aspire to the senior roles, must take part in the succession of 'between seasons' plays. They are the accepted training grounds and are watched attentively by those concerned in the eventual casting of the Passion Play itself.

Many Oberammergauers spend almost half a lifetime on the village stage, starting as child actors and progressing, decade by decade, to the leading roles.

In line with the actors, the orchestra has to be rehearsed, the chorus trained, and the whole vast ensemble integrated into a single, cohesive whole, while in the background, a large staff of wardrobe mistresses must make, renew, renovate or alter more than 1,000 costumes, carpenters and painters replace the worn scenery, stage-hands must assemble the props and electricians service the modern hoists that are used to move the scenery. The cross in the crucifixion scene is hoisted in this manner while the curtains are open. A lighter cross, weighing eighty-five pounds, is used for the scene where it is carried to Golgotha by Christ. The spear that is used is reputed to be more than 300 years old, and when Christ's side is pierced the point automatically disappears and a splash of 'blood' is ejected from the shaft.

Though the Passion Season starts in May and continues until September, the whole of the Passion Year is generally held to be sacred. No dancing nor any public amusements are encouraged, weddings are often postponed to a less 'solemn' year, and every spare moment and thought is devoted to the forwarding of this centuries old enterprise.

As the snows disappear in the spring of that year, the villagers set about renewing the paintwork on their houses, in refreshing the religious frescoes that adorn most of them, cultivating their flower boxes and baskets and spring-cleaning their homes. Shops are filled with the beautifully carved souvenirs, guest houses are newly decorated, cafés re-equipped—and the churches refurbished in anticipation of the mass invasion of visitors.

7 The Passion Theatre

The earliest productions of the Passion Play took place in the parish church. No stage was used, there was no music, and in all probability the performance lasted for only a very short time.

The church was small, built to serve a community of less than 300 souls, and, except for a few merchants in transit through the Ammer Valley, the audience—or congregation—would be confined to those who lived in Oberammergau. But even as early as 1670, interest in the Passion Play was growing, and at the same time the producers were becoming more ambitious, outgrowing the meagre facilities of the village church.

In 1674 the performances were transferred to the cemetery alongside the church and overlooking the mass graves of the victims of the plague, where a makeshift platform was erected—the first step towards the creation of a full-scale theatre, probably unimagined by any of those concerned in that year. It had neither walls nor roof, the floor was bare earth, there were no seats, no dressing rooms and no scenery.

In 1742 a new church had to be built to replace the burned-out structure—burned by the villagers because it was almost in a state of collapse, to clear the site. Though this new edifice was considerably larger than the old it was still inadequate as an auditorium for the Passion Plays.

The next series of plays in 1750 was therefore continued in the open air, but the platform was moved from the cemetery to a nearby field on the direction of Father Alois Plutz, the parish priest of that time. Possibly the priest felt that the play was being taken out of the hands and influence of the church and decided to disown it.

In 1815 a much more serviceable stage was built under the direction of Father Nikolas Umloch, the parish priest and, as it happened, the son of a master carpenter. It was he who first designed the layout of a fore-stage, a centre-stage and wings, permitting a much wider scope for the presentation of the various acts.

The design proved itself to be so effective that when it was decided by the Committee of the Play that an even more ambitiously constructed theatre should be established, in a setting where a much larger audience could be accommodated, it was Umloch who was called back from his new parish of Garmisch-Partenkirchen to design and supervise the new structure.

The site was transferred to a large meadow just clear of the village, known thereafter as the 'Passion Meadow'—where the theatre of today stands. Here Nikolas Umloch built his new stage, larger than the first but still bearing the features of his original design in the fore-stage, centre-stage and the wings—broadly, the design that persists to this day, despite numerous additions and ever more realistic settings.

The new stage was also designed to be readily taken apart and pulled down in sections at the end of each season and re-erected, simply, in time for the next.

But no thought was given to the creation of an auditorium until near the end of the nineteenth century, when a rough lean-to roof, easily dismantled, was put up to shelter a few rows of benches at the back.

Except for minor alterations and the creation of a façade, no further developments were attempted until 1890. It was then that Ludwig Lang, the Director of the School of Carving, with the expert help of Lautenschlager, the stage manager of the Munich Court Theatre, completely redesigned the stage. As soon as the play committee passed the new plans, Breitsamter of Oberammergau was commissioned to do the building.

It was an entirely new construction, massive in concept, though the fundamental designs of Umloch were adapted and broadened rather than abandoned. The houses of Pilate and Annas were removed from their original position in the centre of the stage and separated, broad stairways replaced the original balconies, and two narrow streets were added to improve access to the stage. And for the first time, real thought was given to the creation of a proper auditorium.

The new structure was designed to accommodate an audience of 4,000 under a huge, arched roof—though the stage itself remained, and still remains, uncovered.

The work was finally completed in 1899, in time for the twenty-ninth Passion Play Season of 1900.

Interest in this new theatre became so widespread that the demand for seats for the 1900 season could only be satisfied by forty-six performances. In 1910 fifty-six performances were staged, and in 1922 no fewer than sixty-eight performances had to be given to accommodate the 310,000 visitors. This, despite the shattered economy of Germany as the aftermath of the First World War.

Hopefully, as Germany slowly emerged from the trough of abject poverty in the mid-twenties, the Committee of the Passion Play decided that an entirely new, and permanent construction should be undertaken.

Baurat Hocheder of the Munich Buildings and Works Department designed the project to the requirements of the producer of the play, Georg Johann Lang. Professor Linnebach was called in to design the stage equipment, including electric hoists, situated under the stage, to lift and move the massive scenery necessitated by the forty different settings in which the play is enacted.

This new structure was completed in time for the 1930 season, built of concrete and steel and permanent in character, but by 1934—the tercentenary year—the stage had been broadened and the auditorium enlarged to accommodate over 5,000, in fixed, tip-up seats.

Further reconstruction was carried out in readiness for the 1960 season. The south entrance to the auditorium was rebuilt to give a larger foyer and wide stone stairways replaced the wooden steps. The interior walls were panelled and the seating capacity increased to accommodate about 6,500.

The stage is now a solid construction of stone, concrete and steel. It remains open to the weather and the audience, from under the roof of the auditorium, get a magnificent view of the Bavarian Alps towering in the background behind the stage settings. On occasions, the heavens have roared with thunder and flamed with lightning during the scene where Christ is crucified, creating acute emotional stress among the audience.

On the right and left of the huge stage, there are two streets of Jerusalem. On the extreme left, steps lead up to the platform before the House of Pilate, the Roman Governor, and to the right, similar steps lead to the House of Annas, the High Priest. In front of the stage is a vast well for the orchestra, with facilities for them to shelter under the stage in heavy rain—and behind are the dressing rooms for 700 performers.

There are wardrobe rooms containing a great collection

of robes and uniforms, all of excellent quality, even though a large proportion of them represent the rags of the poor as worn during the few short years of Christ's lifetime. But endurable quality is necessary where the costumes have to withstand the vagaries of the weather on an open stage. Some of the costumes are truly splendid; those of the Speaker of the Prologue, Herod, Annas and Pilate are magnificent.

The props, such as the armour, shields and spears of the Roman soldiers are to be seen hung in rows on the walls—but there are no wigs or false beards.

There are three crosses; that for the criminals, the lighter cross to be borne by Christ on his way to Calvary and that on which He is crucified. The table used in the Last Supper is said to have been constructed in the early part of the eighteenth century and used in every play since.

There are no fewer than 123 speaking parts in the Passion Play, the orchestra has as many as fifty instrumentalists, and the chorus is made up of thirty women and eighteen men. In all, as many as 700 are engaged either on the stage or in the orchestra pit; and almost 1,000 in the multiplicity of service personnel from cleaners, ushers, scene shifters—and so on.

Today Oberammergau has a permanent, modern theatre, designed together with all the ancillary services, for the sole purpose of staging the Passion Play.

Though the modern auditorium is covered in, it is open to the stage and, on occasions, can be draughty. Nor is there any form of heating—and it can be cold in the early mornings in this mountain resort or when the sun is hidden by clouds or rain. Visitors will find that the seats are unpadded and cushions are very necessary—each performance lasts from 8.30 in the morning until about midday and continues from 2 p.m. until six in the evening.

There are no cloakrooms and no place to deposit clothing or other articles. Opera glasses, or field glasses, are almost a must in that vast auditorium, but there is no difficulty about hearing the actors. The panelling of the auditorium is constructed in such a way that it will neither reflect nor absorb the sounds from the stage—and no microphones are necessary to carry the voices of the players even as far as the back rows.

The taking of photographs is forbidden, and, bearing in mind that the people of Oberammergau and very many of the visitors look upon the Passion Play as more of a religious service than an entertainment, smoking is prohibited, and every member of the audience is expected to be in his or her place before the Speaker of the Prologues steps out onto the stage.

8 Oberammergau Today

Oberammergau changed but little during the first century after the plague. It remained a tiny, inaccessible community, uninfluenced by the outside world. Politics barely touched it; indeed there were times when its citizens did not even know who was their titular ruler. News came to them via the mountain passes, late or not at all, and the 'rights conferred on them, by Ludwig the Bavarian to administer their own affairs left them coldly disdainful of the peasant villagers beyond their valley—and completely uninterested in the government in Munich. Even the never-ending succession of wars that bedevilled Bavaria seemed to roll around and past them, yet never through the Ammergau.

But these conditions were not to last; no community could remain for long in a vacuum as the upsurge of industry, the need for trade routes and a dawning education began to create a widening field of interests, both inside and outside the valley. And, above all else, the desperate need of governments to garner taxes from every possible source to support national armies and the encroachments of rapacious mercenaries left but few habitations to their own devices.

Yet, despite an unwilling emergence from obscurity

into the life of Europe, the Passion Play continued to be very much the private concern of the inhabitants of Oberammergau—until the coming of the railway put an end to their splendid isolation. Thereafter, as swiftly as the story of the Passion Play spread abroad and the lengthening tracks eased the burden of the journey for those who were eager to see it, so the tide of visitors swelled—eventually to massive proportions.

Nor were the people of Oberammergau slow to take advantage of this flood of visitors. Few would deny that the present scale of the Passion Play far exceeds both the letter and the spirit of the vow taken more than 300 years ago, and the bandwagon tactics of the hoteliers, restaurateurs, woodcarvers and the proprietors of every other sort of commercial enterprise designed to facilitate the stay of—or should it be, 'to batten on'?—the visitors, has caused them to prosper exceedingly.

The unprecedented increase in the population of the village during the present century has done much to swamp the descendants of the few survivors who stood in the village church to pray for deliverance from the plague, in 1633, and perhaps the business acumen of some of these newcomers has rubbed off onto the older families.

In 1939, the year of the outbreak of the Second World War, Oberammergau had a population of 3,200—today, some thirty years later, that number has swollen to more than 6,500. But among the present inhabitants it is estimated that less than 4,000 can trace their family history in Oberammergau back for more than a single generation—twenty-five years.

It was the aftermath of the Second World War that doubled the population of the village—in a nation that had lost 5,000,000 on the battlefield in six years, and had destroyed another 5,000,000 during purges and in concentration camps.

But once again, Oberammergau had escaped the worst of the ravages of war, sunk in its mountain fastness; no battle was fought in the Ammer Valley and no Allied air raids came to wreck the village.

To this haven many hundreds of displaced persons, refugees from Eastern Germany, bombed out families and stateless wanderers, came in search of shelter and food and in the main, were welcomed and succoured. Many of these newcomers soon found employment, working for the American Occupation Forces, who established vast recreational centres for their troops in or near the village. They built blocks of flats for the families of their soldiers, shopping precincts—and generally created a tide of prosperity. And with the N.A.T.O. agreement to maintain American Forces in Germany, this huge centre continues to provide a substantial amount of business and employment for the old and the new citizens of Oberammergau.

The massive growth of tourism in the district even created a labour shortage—and, no doubt, as the problem of additional housing is met, so will the number of immigrants into the village increase.

Oberammergau has long been a centre for woodcarving, and today this particular industry is of first importance to its prosperity. A State School of Woodcarving was opened in the village in 1888 to ensure that the quality of its craft should continue to bear a high reputation amongst the world's buyers.

The origin of the craft in the village is not known with any certainty, but as the lay brothers of Rottenbuch Monastery carried the art to Berchtesgaden in 1111, it would seem probable that it even preceded the erection of Ettal Monastery in the Ammer Valley.

The craftsmen of Oberammergau certainly fell under the influence of the monks and concentrated their art on religious carvings. This influence has endured, and the craftsmen have always been noted for their portrayals of Christ on the Cross, the saints and such large set-pieces as Christ in the manger, and larger-than-life Madonnas— and, alternatively, tiny crucifixes and figures of the saints.

There is a museum in the village. It was founded in 1906 by the then Councillor of Commerce, Guido Lang and acquired by the community in 1954. It contains a rich collection of carvings, some taken from the old church and others given by private owners. Some of the carvings date back to the fourteenth century, in particular, a precious figure of the Holy Barbara. There are paintings, both on canvas and on glass, some of which depict the Stations of the Cross.

Toys abound in one room and another is full of toy soldiers. Modern exhibits in pewter and plastic are on exhibition, and there are even mechanical soldiers to be seen. The principal attraction of the 'toy room' is a model of the capture of the fortress of Scharnitz by the French, containing no fewer than 300 soldiers.

Antique furniture, some of it no doubt originating in the Ettal Monastery, fills another room and includes such treasures as figures of Bacchus and of Mercury, clock-cases, goddesses and pastoral scenes.

There are, in all, nine exhibition rooms in the museum wherein are displayed many items of the woodcarvers art, such as the 'Munich October Festival 1825', the Boy Jesus in the Temple and the Last Supper.

In Number 5 Daisenberger, the house of Georg Lang— for so very many years the director and producer of the play—there is on show a beautifully carved Christmas crib. The craftsmanship is superb and includes a number of tiny figures, jointed and dressed, to portray some of the costumes and the actors to be seen on the stage of the Passion Theatre. It is a devotional work of first importance and took eighty years to complete—from 1780 to 1860.

Tourism is the principal feature of Oberammergau during the inter-season years, and in its beautiful setting, deep in the dense forests and among the towering mountains of southern Bavaria, there lies an enchanting alternative to the 'brassy' resorts that proliferate the Mediterranean coastline. Its situation in the Ammergau Valley, 2,500 feet above sea level, ensures deep, unsullied snow, crisply clean air and exciting ski-runs during the winter—and, in the summer, long, warm days in a crystal-clear atmosphere that makes mountaineering and sightseeing a refreshing delight.

It was in 1886 that the first serious attempt was made to put Oberammergau on the tourist maps of the world. Pleasure gardens and promenades were created and a general 'tidying up' of the village added much to the attraction provided by the Passion Plays. So much so that it was not long before these new amenities began to encourage a flow of visitors in the years between the Passion Seasons.

In 1931 the community of Oberammergau took over the work and expanded the original concept. A large open-air swimming pool was built in the St. Gregor district. The main pool is immense, measuring 330 feet by 130 feet, and nearby are two smaller pools, one for the few women who still prefer privacy and the other for children. The water is warmed before it flows into the pools and is replaced at the rate of 900 gallons every minute, keeping the temperature at a constant 66 degrees fahrenheit —and free from dirt and windblown leaves.

Diving towers, water-chutes and other amenities border the pools—the whole are surrounded by beautifully kept lawns, flower beds and shady spots under trees. There are facilities for sun-bathing, and the children are provided with sand-pits and paddling pools. There are garden terraces—and the most hygienic of changing rooms.

Near the pools stands the valley station of the Laber Mountain Cable Car, which was opened in 1957. This cable railway climbs to the top of the mountain, 5,610 feet above sea level, and there is a large, glass-walled restaurant at the top from which there is a truly magnificent view of the rugged mountain scenery.

Ski-ing, is of course, one of the chief winter attractions, and there are two ski-lifts on the slopes of the Kolben—together reaching 1,000 feet up the mountain side. There is a long, international standard run from the cable car terminal on the Laberjoch, and there are nursery slopes in plenty. And, so that the veriest novice can learn to enjoy the sport, there is a ski-school in the village.

Close to the Passion Theatre there are tennis courts readily adaptable in the winter into ice rinks, and, for those of the visitors who expect to see religious drama even outside the Passion Season, the Kleines Theatre—Little Theatre—provides an unending series of plays, usually referred to as 'training plays', though each of them is a highly skilled performance.

It is in such plays as these that aspiring Passion Play actors make their debut—and it is quite the thing for visitors to try and pick out those of them who are likely to achieve success. On the stage, too, there are actors who have already gained recognition and even fame, but who need to keep their art alive during the fallow decades between the Passion Seasons.

One of the most attractive features of Oberammergau are the exquisitely painted frescoes on each and every building. They are invariably of a religious character, depicting some incident in the life of Christ, or one or more of the saints. Some of these colourful adornments were originally painted decades earlier and, except for retouching, have never been altered. Many of the village houses still stand as they did a century or more ago—externally, at any rate—but unfortunately the American influence since 1945, has too often brought about conversions to a more modern, 'plate glass and stainless steel' glossiness. Shops are taking on a supermarket atmosphere, restaurants are being given a slick-service appearance, and the blocks of flats built as married quarters for their troops, look intensely alien.

The same influence and the array of continually changing fashions brought in by the tourists, has tended to consign the traditional dress of the local people to obscurity, too. Rarely now, except on festive occasions, do we see the men of Oberammergau in their lederhosen—leather shorts with richly embroidered braces—a white shirt with a colourful silk scarf about their necks, a green felt hat with a 'shaving brush' of eagle's plumage in the band and gaudily knitted calf stockings. The girls wear, on High Days, crisply frilled blouses, colourful dirndl skirts supported by an ample supply of lace-hemmed, well-starched petticoats. Their shoes are black and flat-heeled, adorned with enormous silver buckles and their hair is built up in a series of plaits.

The parish church was completed in 1742 and replaces the old Gothic structure that almost crumbled into dust before it was pulled down. The crucifix of the Altar of the Cross is, however, a survival from that older church.

The paintings in the two domed vaults are by Matthias Ginther, one time Director of the Augsburg Academy, and are dated 1741 and 1746. They represent 'The Apostles, Peter and Paul, taking leave of one another', 'The Crucifixion of Peter' and the 'Beheading of Paul'. The centre-piece depicts the martyrs being received by a host of saints. There are a large number of other paintings by Ignaz Paur and again by Ginther, and the sculptor Xaver Schmaedl is responsible for the intricately carved wood-work of the High Altar and much else in the church besides.

Masses are celebrated in the church from as early as 5 a.m. preceding each of the Passion Plays. There is a Protestant Church too, adjacent to the Passion Theatre, where morning and evening services are conducted in both German and in English—and where an organ recital is given, every day of the play, during the luncheon interval between midday and 2 p.m.

To cater for the ever increasing flow of visitors to the village and its play, there is a railway service nowadays that covers the sixty-mile journey to and from Munich in about an hour and a half. From there, international trains, with all the modern amenities of restaurant and buffet cars, sleepers and couchettes, speed directly to every major city in Europe – and beyond. Buses cover the surrounding area, including Berchtesgaden and Hitler's infamous mountain retreat in the Bavarian mountains, Würzburg, Augsburg, Lindau and across the border to the Austrian city of Innsbruck. There is a service to Munich-Riem airport that connects with regular flights to all parts of the world.

The network of roadways through the mountains includes an autobahn from Munich, to within a few miles of Oberammergau and a good road from there on.

9 The Story of Christ's Passion

The Feast of the Passover was at hand and from far and near the pilgrims turned their footsteps towards Jerusalem. Thousands upon thousands of them travelled in great caravans, on the backs of donkeys or on their bare feet; they crossed the wide seas, the high mountains and the arid deserts on the great trek to celebrate the annual feast that commemorated the long ago Exodus of the Israelites from Egypt.

And among the great crowd of hurrying pilgrims, Jesus strode along in company with His twelve disciples.

As soon as they entered the city, Christ made for the Temple, strode inside—and stood in angry silence as He saw the concourse of traders that filled the great hall.

Stalls loaded with trade goods covered the floor and were surrounded by shoppers, caged birds hung from the canopies on offer to any would-be buyer, and the money-changers, each with his abacus and tablets, were busily reaping a rich reward for themselves by converting the coins of many lands into local currency.

The Temple resembled nothing so much as a public market place.

Jesus turned on the traders. He overturned the tables of the money-changers, upset the stalls and scattered their contents across the floor. He threw aside the chairs of those who sold doves and drove the merchants out into the street, calling after them, "It is written, My house is the house of prayer; but ye have made it a den of thieves."

For seven days afterwards Christ was left in peace to preach to all those who would listen to Him, and word quickly passed around the city that the miracle-man of Galilee was amongst them. As the news spread of the cures He was effecting, the lame, the sick and the blind began to flock to the Temple to beg Him to help them.

The children were not slow to infiltrate the crowds that forced their way into the Temple, curious to see what was going on. So enthralled were they by the stories He told them that they stayed on to watch the miracles. They fell into a spellbound silence each time the Healer laid His hands on a cripple and cheered wildly as the cripple walked away. Gangs of them raced through the narrow, tortuous streets of the city, crying the news—and scurried back again in case they should miss some new wonder.

But far less pleased, of course, were the traders who had been driven from their favourite market place in the Temple, to set up their stalls again in the hot, dusty streets. Nor were the priests of the Temple any better pleased to note that this new prophet from Nazareth was turning the crowds away from their traditional religious leaders towards Himself.

The traders and the priests put their heads together in an attempt to find some way of discrediting Jesus and to silence Him, but it seemed that the crowd were much too intent on the revelations of the new teacher to be swayed by anything that could be said against Him—and too appreciative of His miracles to be persuaded to oust Him from the Temple.

The priests tried to silence the children, but failed dismally. Then they hit upon the idea of sending their servants and the Temple guards out into the streets to encourage a storm of protest against the prophet among those who had not yet seen Him and had not, therefore, fallen under His thrall.

But it was very soon obvious to the worried priests that in this way lay the danger of a head-on collision between their own supporters and those of Christ, that could too easily end up in a bloody street battle—with no assurance that their own faction would carry the day.

Worriedly, the priests withdrew the rabble-rousers again and commenced new talks with the traders. The discussions went on for a long time before the decision was reached to ask the Sanhedrin—the Council of the High Priests—to bring the whole weight of the law down on Christ's head.

But while they still argued, Jesus with his disciples, withdrew to Bethany.

Caiaphas was the High Priest of the Temple and it was he who called the chief priests, the scribes, the traders and the elders of the city before him to a session of the Sanhedrin.

He told the gathering of his fear that, left too long a free man, Christ would usurp the dignity of the High Priests and lay claim to rule in the Temple of Jehovah. He warned them that the next step would be the overthrow of the Law given to Moses by God, the abolition of the religious fasts, the banning of sacred sacrifices and the profaning of the Sabbath. And, perhaps pertinently, of God's priests being divested of their offices.

The traders too, had their say. They pointed out that with the vast influx of visitors to Jerusalem for the Feast of the Passover, there was little time to waste in dealing with the crisis posed by the upstart prophet if they were yet to gain the fullest advantage of the season's business.

A priest then demanded that Christ should be seized and imprisoned, another that it should be done in secret so that the people should know nothing about it.

But one thing was evident to the assembly; whatever action they decided to take, it must be done quickly and before the Passover if they were not to risk an enormous outcry against the sullying of that day.

The decision was then made to arrest Jesus—but there remained the problem of finding Him and identifying Him to the guards who would be sent to take Him.

Dathan, one of the traders, assured the council that he knew one of Christ's followers who could be bribed to betray Him.

Caiaphas promised to provide the necessary bribe from the Temple treasury and Dathan agreed to approach the disciple whom he hoped would pin-point Jesus for the guards.

Jesus spent the night in Bethany, but He chose to stay in the house of Simon the leper—whom He had cured of his leprosy—rather than with his friends, Mary Magdalene, Martha and their brother Lazarus.

The date was 1st April in the year A.D. 30.

Yet it was Martha who was asked to cook and serve the supper that was to be got ready for Christ, His disciples and Lazarus—who were to sit together at the same board.

During the meal Mary Magdalene suddenly appeared bringing with her an alabaster vase filled with a fine and expensive ointment. She had spent all that she and her sister had saved on it for the burial of Lazarus, whom Christ had raised from the tomb. She was determined to expand it on Christ in token of her gratitude for the deliverance of her brother.

She knelt and bathed the feet of Jesus in the sweet

smelling ointment and dried them with her long hair. She then poured more of the precious oil over His head.

One of the disciples, Judas Iscariot, son of Simon their host, looked shocked. He was the purse-holder for the little band of Christ's followers and he was only too well aware of their poverty. He tried to snatch the vase from the hands of Mary, but Jesus stopped him and persuaded Judas to leave the woman alone.

When they had finished their meal Christ rose from the table and told His friends that he was about to return to Jerusalem.

Mary Magdalene did her best to dissuade Him. She told Him that she had a dreadful feeling of doom at the very thought of His return to that city and begged Him to stay away from it.

The disciples were equally disturbed at the prospect, knowing well that the priests were anxious to silence Jesus, and they added their pleas to those of Mary—but Christ was adamant, though he admitted to them that once he left Bethany he never expected to see it again.

Before He left His mother and her friends came to see Him. She too protested at His departure, but Jesus told her that His return to Jerusalem was the will of God, though He knew that in that city he would be parted from them all—probably for the last time.

Early on the morning of the Sunday before the Passover, Jesus led His disciples up the stony road that wound its way up and into the city of Jerusalem.

It was a hot day and a dusty road, and they paused for a while on the slopes of the Mount of Olives. As they rested Jesus called two of his disciples to Him and ordered them to go on ahead of the rest of them to the village of Bethphage, a suburb of the city. There, He told them, they would find tied to a post beside its mother, a colt, that had never yet been ridden by man. They were to loose the ass and to lead it back to Him.

The disciples looked worried at being given an order that suggested that they must steal the beast, but Christ assured them that they need only tell the owner that the Lord had need of it and they would be allowed to take it away unhindered.

The two disciples soon found the colt that Jesus had so surely described to them, standing beside its mother and near to its owners.

They unhitched the young animal and, of course, the owners promptly protested. But as soon as they were told that it was being taken for the Lord's service, they stood to one side—just as Jesus had said they would.

The disciples then led the ass back to where Jesus waited for them, then they threw a cloak across its back—and He mounted it.

There was a great crowd on the road, everybody trudging purposefully towards Jerusalem, and it was not long before Jesus was recognized and the news of His presence amongst them spread like wildfire. He was greeted joyfully; even ecstatically, as many of them re-called that the prophet Zacharias had foretold, centuries before, that "the king comes to you meek and sitting upon an ass".

Happily they urged the donkey and its precious burden forward—but among the travellers there were a number of Pharisees and Sadducees who viewed the greetings that were being showered on Jesus with dismay and even with alarm, and they began to edge their way through and clear of the crowd, with the intention of hurrying on ahead to warn the priests.

They were badly frustrated in their efforts by the crowd that persisted in milling around Jesus and, as its enthusiasm soared, cloaks were spread down in the path of the donkey on which He rode, boughs were lopped from nearby trees and thrown down as a carpet, and wild flowers were plucked, woven into posies and showered on Him. The joyful noise swelled, and the cheering rose to turn the journey into a triumphal progress, but a few of the Pharisees succeeded at last in getting clear of the crowd without attracting unwelcome attention to themselves, and they trotted ahead of the procession.

Slowly, noisily, a little dustily, but with immense joy, the crowd accompanied Jesus and His disciples on their slow trek towards the city until, at last, the great walls, the gate-towers and the protective forts came within sight. Then Jesus paused and gazed at Jerusalem with unexpected tears in His eyes.

Gently and sorrowfully, he foretold what none who heard Him could believe of so great a city:

For the days shall come upon thee, that thine enemies shall cast a trench about thee; and compass thee round, and keep thee in on every side.

And shall lay thee even with the ground, and thy children within thee; and they shall not leave in thee one stone upon another; because thou knowest not the time of the visitation.

Christ then sent two of His disciples, Peter and John, on ahead to prepare the Easter lamb so that it might be eaten that night. When they asked Him where He would stay, He told them that they would meet a water-carrier and that they should follow him to his master's House. There they should ask the householder for the guest-chamber so that they could eat their Passover meal with the Lord in privacy.

Then the joyous procession followed Jesus into Jerusalem where an even greater crowd awaited Him to escort Him to the Temple.

When Jesus led His disciples into the Temple, He warned them that it would be for the last time. But Judas protested, complaining that to leave them now meant that they would be abandoned to their poverty. He begged Jesus to make some provision for their future and reminded Him of the wasted oil that Mary Magdalene had used to anoint Him, that might well have been sold for some substantial sum.

Christ did what he could to assure Judas that he and the rest of His disciples would never lack for enough to satisfy their bodily needs, but he promised no more than that.

Alone, Judas grew deeply despondent about the future; he had hoped that Christ would re-establish the Kingdom of Israel in all its ancient pomp and glory and magnificence, but it seemed that this new king was offering his followers no more than poverty and misery—and for Himself, arrest, imprisonment and death.

The more he thought about it, the less he liked the prospect, until, slowly and with deepening gloom, it dawned on him that the time was not far off when he would betray Jesus.

It was while he was still in this mood that Dathan and others found Judas, and he listened glumly as they questioned him about Christ's movements.

For a time Judas kept the knowledge to himself—perhaps because of some ingrained loyalty; more probably in the hope of being offered a reward in exchange for the information.

With wily astuteness the priests' men expressed their sympathy for the unhappy plight of anyone burdened by poverty, and, as Judas sank even more deeply into the doldrums under the picture they drew for him of his own future as a follower of Christ, they saw that they had shaken his loyalty until it was about to break.

Then they tempted the discontented disciple with the

promise of a rich reward from the Sanhedrin if he would tell them where Jesus was going to spend that night.

Judas kept silent for a while longer—until he was given a quiet hint that crucifixion was likely to be the end for all those who retained their allegiance to the Prophet of Nazareth.

A rich reward—or crucifixion? Judas gave up. He promised to find out where his Master was to stay that night and to bring the news to the Sanhedrin.

Peter and John found a young water-carrier near a street-well in Jerusalem and they followed him to the house of his employer. At their request the youth introduced them to Mark, his master, who recognized them at once as the followers of the Christ who had cured him of his blindness. Mark welcomed them with open arms and when they asked for the use of his guest-chamber, in which Jesus and his disciples wished to celebrate the Passover, he gladly agreed.

Jesus sat down to His Last Supper with His twelve disciples in the upstairs room of Mark's house in Jerusalem.

He knew that His life had almost run its course and again He warned his followers of the event by holding up a cup of wine, giving thanks and offering it to them saying, "I will not drink of the fruit of the vine until the Kingdom of God shall come."

He broke some bread into pieces and gave a portion to each of them declaring it to be His body, and the wine, the blood which he was soon to shed.

Then, when the feast came to an end, Jesus took off his cloak and laid it aside. He filled a bowl with water, gathered up a towel and knelt at the feet of Simon Peter.

Peter protested sharply at the idea that Jesus should wash the feet of any man, least of all his own—but Christ insisted, passing from one disciple to another as he bathed and dried the feet of each of them in turn.

Then, suddenly, he astounded the twelve men by announcing that one of them would betray Him and bring about His death.

There was an immediate uproar of denials, protests and demands to be told who was to be the traitor. Every one of them asked the same question, "Is it I, Lord?"

John laid his head on Christ's shoulder and pleaded, "Lord, who is it?"

Christ held up a piece of bread and told them that it would be he who received it that would be His betrayer.

The silence was deep and intense as Jesus dipped the piece of bread into the gravy that remained with what was left of the Easter lamb—and held it out to Judas Iscariot.

Judas took it tremblingly, and asked, "Is it I, Master?"

"What thou doest, do quickly," Jesus urged him quietly.

In silence and with his head bowed in shame, Judas rose from the table, slipped from the room and left the house.

As they sat around the table deeply troubled, Peter pleaded to be allowed to accompany Christ wherever he should go, or to whatever fate awaited him—and swore that if it was necessary, he would gladly lay down his life at His side.

But Jesus shook His head and told him, gently, "that in this very night, before the cock crows twice thou shalt deny me thrice".

The disciples joined Peter in his urgent, desperate protestations of loyalty to Jesus and demanded that they be allowed to stay with him whatever happened, but Jesus soothed them with the assurance that though He would go alone, it would be to prepare a place for them in Heaven and that He would return for them in due time.

Then He led them from Mark's house and turned His steps towards the Mount of Olives.

The High Priest Caiaphas gave the news of Judas's defection to the members of the Sanhedrin, and a great sigh of relief swept over them. For the news of the growing popularity of the new prophet had worried them badly and they saw their priesthood—a state within a state—about to crumble around them.

Caiaphas wanted to know what they should pay Judas for his treachery, but Nathaniel pointed out, contemptuously, that under the Law of Moses a slave is worth but thirty pieces of silver.

The council wasted no time in argument. So long as it was assured that Christ would be delivered into its hands, they had little interest in His betrayer. Besides, now that Judas had declared himself, he must take what was offered or suffer the indignity of being arrested himself as an accessory to the acts of his Master.

Judas was a morose, discontented man. Ambitious for himself, he had expected great things from the new Messiah; wealth instead of poverty, a great position rather than spiritual kudos and power instead of humility. Yet he found it not at all easy to betray the man who had been his friend and leader for three long years.

He knew too, that Jesus had foreseen His betrayal and was aware of whom His betrayer was to be, yet He had made no move to prevent him leaving the table!

Even Judas Iscariot had to feel some remorse for what he was about to do, and it seemed that some inner compulsion was added to the temptation under which he laboured, to urge him on through the streets of Jerusalem to his melancholy meeting with the representatives of the Sanhedrin.

It was Dathan who presented Judas to the High Council of Priests, presided over by the Lord Annas, High Priest of Jerusalem, but it was Caiaphas who questioned the renegade disciple.

As soon as he had satisfied himself that Judas was in fact one of Christ's followers, he sought to find out why he should want to betray his Master.

Judas found a great deal of difficulty in explaining. He had to admit that he had been a close friend of the prophet from Nazareth during the years he had known Him. He admitted too, that he had always believed in Christ's teachings and had been as anxious as any of His followers to forward the mission—but feeling that nothing was being accomplished; indeed realizing at last that the mission intended no personal triumph for anyone but God Himself, his ardour had cooled.

Judas told the attentive assembly how it had been his duty to act as treasurer to Christ and the small band of His disciples, and of the difficulties he had experienced in making ends meet with the few pence that ever came their way, and of the dawning realization that Jesus had no interest in accumulating wealth, nor of giving any thought to the daily problems of providing food and lodgings— content to leave all such matters to the will of God.

The priests shook their heads disbelievingly and demanded to be told why Christ was not yet riding on the tide of the huge welcome he had received on His entry into Jerusalem, to overthrow the established church—and, indeed, the state.

What was His plan of campaign? When did He intend to rouse the masses to revolt?

Judas tried desperately to explain that Christ had no intention of ever attacking the state, nor, in fact, of encouraging any sort of physical demonstration against His enemies—but he was unable to give them any assurance that He would not persuade the people against the priest-hood.

With some return of his remorse Judas begged the Sanhedrin not to harm Jesus, though he must surely have known that the priests were intent on silencing the prophet and would pay little heed to his plea. In fact, Caiaphas treated the betrayer with some contempt and ignored the request; he had already determined that Christ must die if the priesthood was to be freed from the danger He threatened.

He conferred with Annas in private and between them they decided that once Jesus of Nazareth was in their hands, He should be killed.

Judas was then given his instructions.

He was to find out for certain exactly where Jesus intended to spend the night and then to lead a small party of priests, Pharisees and guards to where they could arrest Him. The whole undertaking, however, was to be delayed until after dark, when the city would be sleeping, so that there would be no witnesses of the deed and no one at hand to oppose them.

When the arrest was made, Judas was told, his part in the affair would be at an end.

Judas agreed, but at first he refused to accept the bribe—perhaps in self-disgust; more probably because he felt that thirty pieces of silver was little enough reward for so dreadful a deed.

But it was soon made plain to him that the Sanhedrin had him well and truly in their power and were not disposed to haggle. If necessary, it seemed that they might well treat him as ruthlessly as they obviously intended to deal with Christ, once they had him in their hands.

Helplessly, Judas accepted the blood-money, and it was then arranged that when the time came for the arrest of Jesus, Judas should identify Him to the guards with a kiss.

Then the Sanhedrin dismissed the renegade disciple with orders to meet the posse at the Bethphage Gate after nightfall and to be prepared then to locate the resting place of the Prophet.

As soon as Judas departed, the problem of what was to be done with Christ, after His arrest, was brought out into the open for discussion.

The decision of the Lord Annas and of Caiaphas to kill Him was not readily endorsed by the assembly. Some pointed out that Christ's mission, however damaging to their authority, posed no threat of physical danger, others reminded the meeting that as Jerusalem was under the rule of Rome, they must obey the laws of their overlords, as interpreted by the Roman Governor of the Province, Pontius Pilate.

The aged Annas had no love for the Roman dominion over Jerusalem, but he was wise enough to understand that there could be some very serious repercussions from that quarter if he failed to give at least some semblance of legality to the way the Sanhedrin dealt with the case against Christ. Its authority was wide, but it fell short of pronouncing the death sentence. That ultimate penalty could only be exacted on the orders of the Governor.

Annas made his decision: as soon as the Prophet of Nazareth was taken and brought before him he would send a message to Pilate in his palace of Antonia, detailing their findings against Christ asserting that he had been found guilty of plotting an insurrection against the state—and demanding the death sentence as the only possible sentence.

Darkness had descended over the still busy and boisterous city as Judas stepped out into the street on his sombre errand.

He noticed, as he approached the city gate, that the small party of guards, Pharisees and priests were already there and waiting for him in evident impatience. He was not at all surprised to see the gate opened to allow them to pass beyond the city walls, despite the lateness of the hour, and he noticed too, that the gate guards eyed him closely as he passed by, as though to make sure that they recognized him again when he returned.

Then Judas led his shadowy escort towards the Mount of Olives and to the place where he knew that Christ would be spending the night, in the Garden of Gethsemane.

The Garden of Gethsemane was in fact a walled-farm-yard, and within its boundaries there was a wine-press well known to the people of the district. But it was secluded behind its walls and made an ideal place for rest and retirement.

In the velvety warmth of the pale moonlight Judas cast around the garden cautiously in the hope of finding Jesus while he slept. He knew that the eleven remaining disciples would be there too, and though he realized that the temple guard was powerful enough to overthrow any opposition, he was miserably anxious to avoid any sort of a struggle.

Silently, he signalled the posse to remain still while he crept forward in the eerie darkness.

At last his attention was attracted by the sound of a low, droning monotone and with cautious footsteps Judas edged his way silently towards it—until he could see the shadowy figure of a man kneeling in prayer.

He paused and heard the quiet words, "O my Father, if it be possible let this cup pass from me: nevertheless not as I will, but as thou wilt."

The solemn voice was unmistakably that of Jesus. As He finished His prayer, He rose to His feet and in the faint light of the wan moon He gazed down at His sleeping disciples as they lay on the ground about Him, wrapped in their cloaks against the night air.

He stooped over Peter, shook him awake gently and chided him for sleeping while danger beset them.

He warned the startled fisherman to keep watch while He prayed. Then Jesus moved to one side and found Himself a place where the shadows were deeper. He knelt and prayed once more.

Still Judas hung back, unwilling and perhaps a little frightened to disturb the Messiah as he communed with God.

Again Jesus rose from His knees, only to see that Peter was again asleep among his fellow disciples. He shook His head over them fondly, knowing that they had had an exciting—even a fearful day. Then He left them and stepped into the shadows where He knelt to continue His prayers.

He remained on His knees for only a little while this time, then He rose to His feet, all His prayers said. He returned to Peter, shook him and whispered into his ear, "Behold, the hour is at hand, and the Son of Man is betrayed into the hands of sinners."

Judas too, heard the words—and knew that the time had come for him to keep his promise to those who had bribed him. Silently, he signalled to the guard and the few that had come with them to witness the arrest. He stepped forward, confronted Jesus and greeted Him, "Hail, Master,"—and kissed Him.

The flurry and clatter of the guards as they saw the signal, disturbed the sleeping disciples, who scrambled to their feet and prepared themselves to defend Jesus. In the mêlée in the moonlight Simon Peter drew a sword and with a swift stroke slashed the ear from one of the attackers, but before the others could gather themselves together to give battle, Jesus cried sharply, "Peter, put up thy sword into the sheath."

Shaken by Christ's order, the disciples held back and watched as Jesus held the severed ear of Malchus against the Pharisee's face—and it was healed on the instant.

Then, despairingly, the eleven disciples turned away and scurried off into the darkness, leaving the guards to grab Jesus and to bind his wrists so that he could not escape.

The Lord Annas waited in some considerable anxiety for news of the capture of Christ, and he sent scouts to the city gates to bring him tidings the moment the posse returned. He had not long to wait before Edras came running back to tell him that the party had already re-entered Jerusalem. And almost on his heels, Christ was brought to the house of the High Priest of Jerusalem and taken into his presence.

Christ's wrists remained bound, and Annas had no hesitation in dismissing the guard. Then he listened to Balbus, one of the Pharisees who had witnessed the event, who told him of the capture and of how the disciples had abandoned their leader and fled.

Annas sighed his satisfaction at the success of the enterprise; his judgement had been vindicated too. All that had been necessary to scatter Christ's disciples was His arrest. Now, he could hope that the Nazarene's supporters in the city would just as readily desert their fallen Messiah and quickly forget Him and His teachings.

But when one of the Pharisees, who had seen the incident, told how Malchus had lost an ear in the skirmish and how Jesus had taken the ear and replaced it so miraculously that it had healed at once, Annas began to tremble with anger as his fears swept back over him again. He realized that such a miracle, once it was known to the people, could do a great deal to enrich their faith in the Prophet Jesus.

He questioned Jesus closely about the event in the hope

of forcing the prisoner to disclaim any such miraculous powers, but Jesus did nothing of the kind; He simply asserted that He was the Son of God and had the right to preach as He saw fit.

Angrily, Annas ordered that Jesus should be sent before the Sanhedrin for trial and sentence on a charge of blasphemy.

The moment the decision was taken the doors of the house were flung open, and the little crowd that had gathered outside clamoured for news.

Among them, Judas had waited, full of forebodings, and the moment he learned what Annas had decided, he flung himself forward to protest, reminding Annas of his promise that no harm should come to Christ after His arrest.

A guard hauled the overwrought disciple away and then dragged Christ through the streets towards the house of Caiaphas, the High Priest of the Temple, where the Sanhedrin was to sit in judgement.

A small group of local people hedged the prisoner and his guard about, mocking the prophet, having been hired in advance to cry out against Jesus if there should be any signs of protest from his followers. But they were not needed. In the darkness of the still early hours of the morning and in the narrow, winding streets, few noticed the small procession.

Unseen by Jesus, and unrecognized by the guards, Peter and John mingled with the jeerers, and Peter even succeeded in slipping into the council chamber with those who were being admitted to see the trial.

No fewer than seventy priests assembled to act as judges, and to one side of the chamber there was gathered a small crowd of citizens who had undertaken to give evidence against Christ. The main hall was then filled to capacity with sightseers, almost all of whom had been checked in advance to make sure that they intended to support the judges, whatever their verdict should be.

When Joseph Caiaphas finally took his seat in the assembly, wearing his purple and gold cloak of office, Jesus of Nazareth was arraigned before the most powerful court in the land, subject only to the authority of the Roman Governor of the Province. And it was under the Laws of Moses that the prisoner was to be tried for blasphemy—matters in which Rome tried to keep apart.

The accusers were heard in turn. Nun testified that Christ publicly derided the Sanhedrin as a body of hypocrites; Eliab told how He advised the people not to pay tribute to Caesar; and Gad explained how Jesus spent His time in company with publicans and sinners—hardly blasphemies. But Nun went on to insist that Christ was in the habit of breaking the Sabbath; Gad complained that the false prophet asserted His right to forgive sins; and Eliab spoke of the way He had put Himself above Father Abraham.

Others joined in the chorus of accusation. Raphin told the assembly how Christ had claimed that He could destroy the Temple and rebuild it again within three days, and Eliezer agreed that he too, had heard that blasphemous boast.

No evidence was brought forward in defence of the Nazarene, and Christ was left to answer alone the questions put to Him by the judges.

But Jesus made no attempt to speak in his own defence and remained silent until Caiaphas demanded, "Art thou Christ, the Son of the Blessed?"

To this Jesus replied, "I am."

Caiaphas had no further need to urge the court to find the prisoner guilty. The seventy judges, who were also the jury, promptly demanded His death.

Judas, waiting in the street outside to hear the decision of
the assembly, heard the roar inside the building and,
guessing at the cause, forced a way inside. He cried out
above the uproar demanding to know the judgement—
and was told, as he had already guessed, that the sentence
of the court was 'death'.

Judas protested vociferously, until Caiaphas ordered him
to speak only with respect before the assembled priests.
But Judas was rapidly becoming so angry that no authority
could put a leash on his tongue. He argued wildly that
Christ had committed no crime and demanded his release.
Being wholly ignored by the judges, he threw down the
handful of silver that had been given him as a bribe to
betray Jesus, reviling the Sanhedrin for its injustice, its
dishonourable conduct and lack of mercy.

So vehement was he that Caiaphas ordered his removal
from the building and Judas was taken by the guards and
thrown into the streets, still cursing the judges wildly, the
High Priest with biting anger—and himself, pitiably.

Judas stumbled away at last, thrust a passage for himself
through the crowd that surrounded the house of judgement and headed blindly for the open fields among the
hills beyond the city.

There, he found a rope, chose a convenient tree and—
alone—hanged himself.

The scattered silver was collected and brought to
Caiaphas as he still sat in his seat of judgement, but as it
was blood-money it could not be returned to the temple
treasury. It was suggested that it might most appropriately
be used to buy an acre of land as a burial place for strangers.
The motion was agreed, almost without discussion.

But the assembly had not yet finished its deliberations.
Though it had sentenced Christ to death, the members
were well aware that it was still possible for any number of
Christ's followers to appeal to Pontius Pilate, and they

feared that, being a Gentile, the Roman Governor might well revoke the sentence of a Jewish court.

Caiaphas proposed that the best thing they could do would be to simply take their sentence on Christ to Pilate for confirmation—from whom there could be no appeal. But it must be done at once, he insisted, so that the sentence could be carried out before any opposition could be mounted against them.

The problem was debated long into the night, and in the meantime, in a room at the back of the house, members of the temple guard and some of their friends, sought warmth and a place to take their ease as the long hours dragged by. And among them Peter found a haven as he waited in secret and in despair to hear the final outcome of the trial of Jesus.

Unexpectedly, a young maid suddenly took Peter by the arm, swung him round to face her and then claimed, loudly, that she had seen him before in the company of Jesus.

Peter the fisherman denied the fact hurriedly, but shortly afterwards a man too, declared that he had seen him with the Nazarene. Again the disciple denied the charge, but an hour later yet a third insisted that he was one of Christ's associates.

Peter retorted, "Man, I know not what thou sayest," and almost as the words passed his lips, he heard the crow of a cock.

It was not until the early hours of the morning that a decision was taken to send a deputation to the palace without any further delay, to seek an audience for Caiaphas with the Governor, in order that he could put the case of Jesus of Nazareth before him and obtain confirmation of the sentence passed on Him by the Sanhedrin.

Three representatives of the council were chosen to

make the approach to Pilate, and they set out at once, even though the dawn had hardly broken over Jerusalem.

But on the way, it suddenly occurred to them that, as Jews, they could not enter the house of a Gentile at this season without making themselves unclean. Worriedly, but unwilling to turn back and risk abuse from the High Priest, they decided to carry on to the palace and there to ask one of the Governor's servants to convey the Sanhedrin's request to Pilate.

Pontius Pilate, though a disappointed man in the poor governorship that was his, was astute and well aware of what was going on around him and he was waiting, despite the hour, for the arrival of the deputation from the council. When his servant, Quintus, came to him with their request, he sent him back with a message to say that he was ready at any time to hear the case of Jesus of Nazareth.

Despite the all-night session of the Sanhedrin, so impatient were the priests to have done with Christ that the moment their representatives returned from the palace with the news that Pilate was ready to receive them, they ordered the guards to make sure that their prisoner was properly bound and then to follow the senior members of the council with him, to the palace.

It was still early morning, but the temple servants had had plenty of time to whip up in the streets an even greater throng of those who would support the Sanhedrin and clamour for the sentence to be confirmed and carried out, in the hope of influencing the Governor.

Pilate waited for the arrival of the priests and the condemned man outside the main entrance to his palace—as a concession to the religious scruples of those who wished to plead before him. And when the party arrived he took his place on the high platform he used to overlook those in the courtyard below.

He saw with some impatience that Christ's journey through the streets had been accompanied with more than mere threats and imprecations; there was every sign of ill-treatment about the bound Man. His face was bruised, His robe torn and blood-stained, and the long rope that had been used to drag Him through the streets bespoke rough handling even by the guards.

There was little that Pilate could do about that, but his voice was sharp when he called Caiaphas forward to state his case against the prisoner.

Caiaphas demanded that the death sentence passed on Jesus of Nazareth be confirmed, and when the Governor insisted on being given the reason for such a sentence, the High Priest was impertinent enough to state that had the prisoner not been guilty of some offence He would not have been brought before the Governor.

Pilate refused to accede to any such request until he knew what crime had warranted the sentence, and when he was told that Christ had blasphemed against the holy Laws of Moses, he shrugged and decided that such a parochial affair was a matter for the Sanhedrin to deal with in accordance with their own laws.

Caiaphas told the Governor that all this had been done, but reminded him that no sentence of death could be carried out unless it was confirmed by Caesar's representative in Jerusalem.

Annoyed, Pilate then warned the priests that he would not confirm any sentence of death until he had heard the full details of the crime and had had the opportunity to assess the rightness of the penalty for himself.

Impatiently, Caiaphas then explained that Christ had called Himself the Son of God and King of the Jews, but Pilate saw no crime in such a claim. He saw no wrong in His teachings, nor any harm in His ministry. In fact, he stated flatly that the Nazarene deserved the highest praise for the miraculous cures he was said to have performed.

Caiaphas then switched his attack by accusing Christ of plotting against the state in setting Himself up as an even greater king than Caesar, of urging the people to refuse to pay tribute to the Roman Emperor and as King of the Jews to persuade them to transfer their loyalty from the distant ruler to Himself.

Still Pilate could not be persuaded to credit the stories he was told by the priests. The Christ that stood before him—tattered, weary, bruised and of no authoritative stature—hardly seemed to him to give any sign of kingship—or to be in any way a danger to the realm.

But the priests persisted, and wearily the Governor decided to examine the Nazarene in private, where he could hear His side of the case without the angry arguments of the priests and the noisy crowd that cried their slogans in the background to drown out His words.

Pilate stepped back into the palace, and one of the Roman guards took charge of the prisoner and led Him indoors and into the presence of the Governor.

Pilate questioned Jesus closely and with a great deal of sympathy, but the prisoner would make no real effort to defend Himself. When He was asked if He did in fact claim to be King of the Jews, Jesus neither affirmed nor denied the charge. He simply insisted that His kingdom was not of this world and that all power was in the hands of God.

The examination was interrupted by Quintus, Pilate's servant, who brought him an urgent message from his wife, Claudia Procula.

Patiently, Pilate ordered that Christ be taken into an inner courtyard while he read the message. Claudia's letter was a strange plea that her husband should have nothing to do with any accusation against Jesus, for she had dreamed that he was a good man and that no good would come of any interference with His affairs.

As it happened, Claudia's urgent request was entirely in line with Pilate's own sympathies and he sent his servant back with a promise that she should have no fear of any injustice on his part.

The Governor then called Jesus back into his presence and questioned Him further. But, as before, Christ made no attempt to defend Himself or to deny any of the stories concerning Himself that had been used against Him. He merely told the Governor that even he had no power over Him, except that given him by God.

With a vague understanding of Christ's philosophy, and a deeper knowledge of the forces at work behind the minds of the priests, Pilate's sympathies were all with Jesus, but the Prophet gave him no real grounds for denying the request of the Sanhedrin. Nor was he unaware of the sort of picture of Christ's 'imperial' claims would create in the mind of Caesar, if the priests leaked the story to Rome.

He sighed heavily, returned to the balcony and ordered Christ to be taken out again where they could both be seen and heard by His accusers.

A roar of greeting met Pilate and a welter of abuse swelled about the head of Jesus as He stepped into the open.

Pilate waited for silence, still torn between a genuine sympathy for the prisoner and fear for the consequences from Rome if he permitted any laxity in the authority of the Empire.

At last, weakly, almost apologetically, Pilate announced, "I find no fault in Him."

Caiaphas reminded him angrily—and pointedly—that Caesar had promised that the law of the land should be preserved, that Christ had broken that law and warranted punishment under it.

Pilate agreed, but in return he reminded the priest that

it was up to the Sanhedrin to deal with the case—to the limit of its authority, but that he could find no reason to intervene to authorize the death penalty in such a case.

However, his refusal to confirm the sentence was made only tentatively; he was well aware of the pertinency of the half-uttered threats to complain of his conduct to Caesar, and of the dire results that might well back-fire onto his own head if they did.

Then, while the welter of protests continued, it suddenly occurred to Pilate that as Christ came from Galilee, his immediate overlord was King Herod of that land, and it was in Nazareth, in Galilee, that the first of Christ's 'crimes' had taken place.

With a vast sigh of relief, he ordered that Jesus should be taken before Herod for sentence.

As it happened, Herod was at that time in residence in the Asmodean Palace in Jerusalem, on the heights of Xystas, opposite the Temple, and reluctantly, but determinedly, Caiaphas and the chief priests, with Christ still bound and under guard, turned their footsteps in that direction—accompanied by a growing crowd of intrigued and interested spectators out to see the events of the day.

Herod Antipas was a debauched, uproarious man of no decency. Fat, passionate, lewd and short-tempered, he was widely feared. But when he heard that Jesus of Nazareth was about to be brought before him, his usual downright mercilessness was tempered by the memory of an earlier such episode. He recalled how he had had John the Baptist beheaded, had had his head placed on a silver salver and then had made Salome dance before him with it in her hand.

For perhaps the only time in his life, Herod regretted what he had done, and for a year or more afterwards he had almost believed that Jesus of Nazareth was in fact the

Baptist risen from the dead. He had even feared that Jesus was to be the instrument of some mysterious and dreadful revenge that was to be exacted of him for that brutal murder.

Herod had heard too, much about the miracles performed by Christ, and he was intrigued, and a little fearfully, anxious to meet the man face to face, at last.

Herod had long been sodden with drink and was full of wine when Jesus was dragged before him. He gazed at the bound man for a few moments, shocked and surprised to find so unassuming, so humble a person—and decided, with alcoholic laughter that Jesus should perform, there and then, a miracle for him.

But Jesus neither answered him nor made any move to demonstrate his miraculous powers. With rising anger Herod demanded that someone should tell him of the charges against the prisoner.

Caiaphas, angry and bitter at having to plead before a drunken, debauched overlord, told him shortly that Christ was causing sedition amongst the people, of urging them to refuse to pay tribute to Caesar and of claiming to be the Messiah, calling himself King of the Jews.

Herod howled his delight at the accusation, pointing out with slovenly gestures that he himself held that title—and dubbed Christ as being the King of Fools.

He ordered one of his servants to bring from his room one of his most regal robes, then he wrapped it about Jesus in jest and sent a party of his soldiers to escort him from the palace with all the pomp of a departing monarch —and to send Him back to Pontius Pilate.

By the time the tired, frustrated, angry, yet still determined priests arrived back at the Governor's palace, the crowd had grown to truly massive proportions, yet, unlike the mood of the previous days, the general cry was against

Christ. They howled their derision and demanded death for him as they struggled to follow the procession and to get near to the bound prisoner.

Before Caiaphas reached the Castle of Antonia where Pilate resided, he had made up his mind that this time the sentence on Christ *must* be confirmed, and that he would tell the Governor flatly that if it was not he would send a complaint to Rome and a demand that Caesar's representative in Jerusalem should fully implement his duties in preserving the law of the land, as had been promised.

Others of the priests, totally exasperated by the shilly-shally of indecision, declared that they would see to it themselves that the sentence was carried out—and that they would be quite ready to face up to the consequences of their action, confident of Caesar's understanding and mercy.

Again Pilate did his best to placate the priests and pointed out to them that it was evident that even King Herod agreed with him that there was no reason for such a sentence. But, led by Caiaphas, the clamour for confirmation of the death sentence became so violently outspoken that, in a mood of defeat, Pilate hedged his decision.

He looked around him at the vast crowd in the courtyard and then, with a sudden switch in temper, he rounded on the priests and, for all to hear, accused them of hatred and bitterness, and of persecution. And before they could reply, he reminded them that at this season of the year it was the custom to release one prisoner. Besides Christ, he told them, there was another prisoner, Barabbas who lay under sentence of death for murder. Of the two, the crowd was to be allowed to choose which of them should be handed over to them as a free man.

Again the priests demanded that Christ should die for his 'crimes', but their attempts to browbeat the Governor failed. Pilate refused to be diverted from his decision.

Perhaps his promise to his wife had something to do with Pilate's refusal to be forced against his will to heed the demands, maybe a genuine sympathy with the humble Prophet encouraged him—but at the back of his mind there was a niggling fear of the consequences of his action, and because of it he attempted a compromise.

Hopefully, he announced that because of His sins, Jesus would be scourged by the soldiers before the crowd so that they could see that justice had been done. Afterwards, he would put it to the throng of watchers to choose between the gentle Jesus who had been punished, and the murderer Barabbas—and he would abide by their decision and free the man they chose.

Hastily, the priests despatched their own guards and servants to round up every man and woman they could find who they knew would support their cause against Jesus, and told them to instruct each one in the crowd to make as much noise as they possibly could, demanding the death sentence on Christ.

Christ was taken before the crowd, shackled and flogged. The crowd screamed their delight and chanted, "Crucify Him! Crucify Him!"

Pilate looked down on the uproarious crowd, shocked by the totally unexpected demands for the life of the humble, unresisting prophet. He had understood that the crowd worshipped the new Messiah and had given Him a tumultuous welcome on His entry into Jerusalem only a few days earlier. Now—this!

Jesus was revived, his back streaming with blood, and in a mood of jest the soldiers threw Herod's royal cloak about his shoulders again, while two others of them plaited a crown of thorns to place on His head, as the crowd roared, "Hail, King of the Jews!"

Then again they cried out, "Crucify Him! Crucify Him!"

Pilate remained still as it slowly dawned on him that the

violence and the urgent, merciless demands of the mass of people below his balcony had been whipped up by the priests. At last he began to understand the cause of it all; how the teachings of this new Messiah threatened the established religion and the status of its priests.

He sighed heavily. What could he do about it? He shook his head defeatedly; he had given his word that the crowd should have the right to decide which of the condemned men, Christ or Barabbas, should be freed in the traditional manner of the Passover.

Slowly, regretfully, already knowing their answer, Pontius Pilate raised his hand for silence and then demanded the verdict of the crowd.

The mob shrieked their decision—they would have Barabbas set free.

Angrily, bitterly and contemptuously the Roman Governor signalled to one of his servants to fetch him a bowl of water. Then, symbolically, he washed his hands in it, and declared, "I am innocent of the blood of this just person."

Then he ordered Barabbas to be brought out, taken beyond the city walls and released there—never to return to Jerusalem.

Barabbas, grey-haired, shaggy and disreputable, was brought up from the castle dungeons. He blinked in the daylight, glanced around him in bewildered disbelief as he was told the news—and then, with a great grin of relief spreading across his grizzled features, he stumbled forward and shuffled off in the company of his escort towards the city gate.

But the eyes of the crowd were on Jesus as He was taken into the castle and remained on Him until He was lost to sight as he was pushed into the guardroom.

The crowd waited impatiently for the last act of the drama

and among them the chief priests held their places, determined to see that the matter should be ended as had been decreed, in the death of Christ.

At last Jesus emerged from the castle for the last time.

The crowd cheered and jeered—and then watched in some silence as the Prophet of Nazareth shouldered the black, wooden cross on which he was to be crucified on the heights of Golgotha.

Then He stepped forward into the narrow street, two thieves under similar sentence, taking their place in the tiny, hapless procession and bearing their own crosses, immediately behind Him.

The crowd began to murmur as Christ was urged on by the soldiers, struggling through the winding lanes, hedged in by the mob and hounded by the guards. Each time He paused in fatigue, the mob cried out demanding that He be goaded on, and each time He stumbled, they jeered.

Once, as He dragged the heavy, cumbersome cross around a sharp corner, He caught a glimpse of Mary his mother, standing helplessly among the crowd and watching heartbrokenly as He passed by.

Jesus stumbled blindly on—but His strength was almost spent. The scourging, the many hours spent without food and the heavy cross was almost more than He could bear. The guards saw His plight; but it was not compassion that persuaded them to help Him, but the fear that He might die too soon, before the crowd could get its full measure of macabre delight from His sufferings.

One of them saw an unknown Cyrenian, large and powerfully built, in the crowd. He ordered the man out of it and commanded him to take the heavy cross from Jesus and to carry it for Him.

And so Simon the Cyrenian made his brief appearance in history as he strode at Christ's side, carrying the clumsy cross with ease on his strong shoulders, as they wound their way through the steep, narrow streets towards Calvary.

And at last, as the news of Christ's progress towards the scene of His crucifixion spread into every corner of Jerusalem, His many followers in the city turned out to join the mass of onlookers. But by now there was little that they could do to rescue the unresisting prophet from His doom.

At one point along the route, one of them, Veronica, stepped out into His path and with tender solicitude took her veil to wipe the dust-laden sweat from His face, and—it is said—the image of Christ's face was printed indelibly thereafter on the veil.

Beyond the city walls a number of women blocked the way, determined to tell Jesus of their compassion for Him, unafraid of the guards, the priests or of anyone else. But Jesus urged them, "Daughters of Jerusalem! Weep not over me, but weep for yourselves, and for your children."

Three times Jesus stumbled to His knees as the little procession climbed the rough path up the slopes of Golgotha, before the condemned men arrived at last, at the appointed place.

At noon, with the soldiers holding back the crowd, the three crosses were laid on the ground and the trio were persuaded to lie down, each on his own cross. Then, swiftly and with expertise, the workmen stripped the doomed men, drove home the great nails, hoisted the crosses and set the foot of each into the ground.

Then they took Christ's garments and tore them into four parts and shared them out amongst themselves—except for the fine, regal cloak that had been given to Jesus, so mockingly, by Herod; for this, they threw dice to decide who should have it.

And above the head of Christ, a sign was put in

Oberammergau in winter

(*above*) The old theatre with the play in progress

(*below*) The new theatre prepared for another season

Four famous players from the Tercentenary Jubilee Performance as they were in everyday life: (a) Christ – Alois Lang; (b) Saint John – Willy Bierling; (c) Caiaphas – Hugo Rutz; (d) Mary – Anny Rutz

The School of Wood-carving: (*left*) carving on main door; (*below*) student at work

Beatrix Lang, selected to play the Virgin Mary in the 1970 Passion Play.

Helmut Fischer, chosen to play the part of Christ in 1970.

Helmut Fischer as Christ in the scene depicting The Last Supper – 1970.

Hans Jablonka, who also played the part of Christ during various performances of the 1970 Play, together with his sister, Elisabeth, who enacted the role of Maria during several performances.

(*above*) Jesus being carried on a donkey into Jerusalem during the 1970 Play.

(*below*) The Crucifixion scene from the 1980 Play.

place that read, "Jesus of Nazareth, King of the Jews."

The hours of Christ's torment dragged on through the heat of the day, and still the priests mocked and reviled the dying man, challenging Him to use His miraculous powers to step down from the cross—until Jesus prayed for them, "Father, forgive them, for they know not what they do."

In their agony the two thieves called on Jesus to save them all, but He offered them only words of comfort, saying, "Verily I say unto thee, Today shalt thou be with me in paradise."

Through the mists of pain, Jesus saw His mother Mary, Mary the wife of Cleophas and Mary Magdalene, and beside them John. To His mother He called down, miserably, "Woman, behold thy son!"—and urged John to care for her after He had gone.

The darkness of an approaching storm spread over the scene from about the sixth hour and persisted, eerily, until the ninth, when Christ suddenly revived a little and cried out in His agony, "My God, my God, why has thou forsaken me?"

For a time he sank back into the mists again, only to complain a little later that he was thirsty. A soldier dipped a sponge in vinegar and put it to the dying prophet's lips, derisively.

A little while longer He lived on, then He suddenly cried out, "Father, into thy hands I commend my spirit," —and died.

The hour was four o'clock in the afternoon of Friday 7th April A.D. 30.

It was Joseph of Arimathea, with Nicodemus, who begged Pilate for the body of Christ. Receiving it, they hurried to Calvary.

A soldier placed a ladder against the cross and climbed

up it, and to make sure that Jesus was indeed dead, he thrust a spear into His side—and from it there flowed a stream of blood and water.

Christ was taken down from the cross and placed in the arms of His mother. His body was anointed with precious oils and then it was borne away and placed in a tomb among the rocks in Joseph's garden.

Mary Magdalene set about the task of preparing spices, helped by others and then when they were ready, early on the Sunday morning, she and Mary the mother of Jesus, John and Salome returned to the tomb to lay the offering at the feet of the dead Jesus. But when they arrived there, they were shocked to see that the stone covering the entrance had been rolled away.

Bewildered and afraid they went inside—and saw that the body of Christ had gone.

As they gazed around them in dismay and horror, the shining figure of two angels appeared before them in the darkness, and a moment later they saw the figure of a young man sitting on the ground. He told them with gentle assurance that Christ had risen from the dead—and that there was nothing for them to fear.

That same day Jesus appeared to Mary Magdalene, and later, He was seen by the others.

Afterwards He appeared to the eleven disciples as they sat together at their suppers. He chided them for their unbelief and hardness of heart, because they had not believed those who had claimed to have seen Him since he had arisen from His tomb.

And He said to them, "Go into all the world, and preach the gospel to every creature."

"And they went forth, and preached every where, the Lord working with them, and confirming the word with signs following. Amen."

10 *The Passion Play*

The Passion Play is concerned only with the period of Christ's life between His triumphal entry into Jerusalem until the Resurrection. The play depicts the story of Christ's farewell to His Mother, the Last Supper, His betrayal by Judas, His arraignment before Pilate, the scourging and His final condemnation. The play reaches its dramatic heights in the Crucifixion and the Resurrection.

The production is made up of sixteen acts and more than sixty scenes, interspersed by twenty tableaux. Each of the acts is introduced by the prologue and the various tableaux are designed to set the scenes for the events which follow. Each tableaux is of an episode taken from the Old Testament, the purport of which is explained by the chorus and every one of them is symbolic and intended to form a link with the scene from the New Testament that follows.

Throughout the play only three lines of the text are not taken from the Bible; the legend of St. Veronica is introduced into the third scene of the fourteenth act, wherein the saint offers Christ a handkerchief as He passes on His way to Calvary. "O Lord!" she cries, "How Thy face is

covered with blood and sweat! Wilt Thou not wipe it?"
Christ wipes His bleeding brow under the crown of thorns
and returns the handkerchief—indelibly stamped with the
impression of His face. "Compassionate soul!" He thanks
her. "The Father will reward thee."

A Prelude and the Hallelujah form the outer covers of
this massive production.

Each performance of the Passion Play starts at 8.30 in the
morning and continues until 5.30 in the late afternoon,
with only a single break, between midday and 2 p.m. for
lunch. There are no pauses between the scenes and no
intervals between the acts.

In the evening before each of the performances there is a
procession led by a band, called 'The Turkische Musik'.
The procession is led by a coterie of small boys, followed
by the band. After them come many of the actors themselves, followed by a crowd of villagers. Anyone else who
cares to join in as the crocodile wends its way through the
streets of Oberammergau is welcome to do so. It is a
musical and colourful scene; everybody sings, and the
Bavarians wear their traditional costumes for the occasion.

On the morning of the play, many of the Catholic
visitors attend one of the early morning Masses.

THE PASSION PLAY

PRELUDE

1st Tableau: The expulsion of Adam and Eve from the
Garden of Eden.   (*Genesis* 3: 22.)

The Prologue welcomes the audience.

2nd Tableau: The Adoration of the Cross.

Part I of the Play covers the action from Christ's entry into Jerusalem, to His arrest in the Garden of Gethsemane.

ACT 1
Jesus in Jerusalem

Scene 1: Jesus enters Jerusalem amidst the acclaim of the crowd.

Scene 2: He drives the traders and money-changers from the Temple.

Scene 3: He departs for Bethany.

Scene 4: The crowd cry, "Moses is our Prophet."
(*St. Matthew* 21: 12–17; *St. Mark* 11: 15–19; *St. Luke* 19: 45–48.)

ACT 2
The Sanhedrin in Council

Tableau: The sons of Jacob conspire against their brother Joseph. (*Genesis* 37: 18.)

Scene 1: Nathaniel complains to the Council about the Galilean.

Scene 2: The traders come to add their complaints.

Scene 3: The High Priests, having ordered the apprehension of Jesus, rejoice.
(*St. Matthew* 26: 3–5; *St. Mark* 14: 1–2; *St. Luke* 22: 1–2.)

ACT 3
The leave-taking at Bethany

1st Tableau: The departure of Tobias from the home of his parents. (*Tobias* 5: 32.)

2nd Tableau: The bride laments the loss of her bridegroom. (*Song of Solomon* 6.)

Scene 1: Christ at Bethany.

Scene 2: Mary Magdalene anoints Jesus.
Scene 3: Judas murmurs against the waste of oil.
Scene 4: Jesus takes leave of His Mother.
(*St. Matthew* 26: 6–13; *St. Mark* 14: 3–9; *St. John* 12: 1–9.)

ACT 4
Christ's last journey to Jerusalem

Tableau: King Ahasuerus of Persia rejects Vashti and the Hebrew maiden, Esther, is chosen as his Queen.
(*Esther* 1: 2.)

Scene 1: Christ goes with His disciples to Jerusalem.
Scene 2: Judas reproaches Jesus for leaving his followers.
Scene 3: Judas meditates on his Master.
Scene 4: Judas is tempted to betray his Master.
Scene 5: Baruch is told that Jesus and His disciples will celebrate the Passover in his house.
(*St. Matthew* 21: 1–11; *St. Mark* 11: 1–14; *St. Luke* 19: 28–44; *St. John* 12: 12–19.)

ACT 5
The Last Supper

Tableau: Moses calls down manna from Heaven.
(*Exodus* 16.)

Scene 1: Jesus washed the feet of His disciples and declares that He will be betrayed by one of them.
Scene 2: Judas departs, Peter declares his loyalty and Jesus leads them towards the Mount of Olives.
(*St. Matthew* 26: 17–30; *St. Mark* 14: 12–26; *St. Luke* 22: 7–34; *St. John* 13 to 17).

ACT 6
The Betrayal

Tableau: Joseph is sold by his brethren for twenty pieces of silver.   (*Genesis* 37.)

Scene 1: Judas is brought before the Sanhedrin.

Scene 2: Judas promises to deliver Jesus into the hands of the Pharisees in exchange for thirty pieces of silver.

Scene 3: The Council decide that Jesus shall die.

Scene 4: The Sanhedrin seek ways to make the death sentence legal.

(*St. Matthew* 26: 14–16; *St. Mark* 14: 10–11; *St. Luke* 22: 3–6).

ACT 7
The Garden of Gethsemane

1st Tableau: Adam must earn his bread by the sweat of his brow. (*Genesis* 3: 17.)

2nd Tableau: Amasa is murdered by Joab.
(2 *Samuel* 20: 9.)

Scene 1: Judas leads an armed band in search of Jesus.

Scene 2: Jesus in agony in the Garden of Gethsemane.

Scene 3: An Angel encourages Jesus.

Scene 4: Jesus betrayed by the kiss of Judas.

(*St. Matthew* 26: 37–56; *St. Mark* 14: 33–50; *St. Luke* 22: 39–51; *St. John* 18: 1–10.)

Part II of the Play tells of the arrest of Jesus in the Garden of Gethsemane, to His condemnation by Pilate.

ACT 8
Christ before Annas

Tableau: The Prophet Micaiah receives a blow for telling Ahab the truth. (1 *Kings* 22: 24.)

Scene 1: Annas waits impatiently for news of the arrest of Jesus.

Scene 2: Judas is horrified to learn that Jesus is to die.

Scene 3: Jesus is brought before Annas.

Scene 4: The mob leads Christ towards Caiaphas's palace.

Scene 5: Peter and John try to discover what has happened to Jesus. (*St. John* 18: 12–13.)

ACT 9
Christ before the High Priest

1st Tableau: Naboth is condemned to death by false witness. (1 *Kings* 21: 8.)

2nd Tableau: Job suffers insults from his wife and friends. (*Job* 2: 9.)

Scene 1: Caiaphas assures the Sanhedrin that Christ is to be condemned.

Scene 2: Jesus is sentenced to death.

Scene 3: Judas casts his blood money before the High Priest.

Scene 4: Caiaphas decides that Jesus must be taken before Pilate.

Scene 5: Pilate agrees to hear the petition of the High Council.

Scene 6: Peter denies Christ.

Scene 7: Peter is penitent.

Scene 8: Jesus is followed and mocked by the crowd.

(*St. Matthew* 26: 57–75 to 27: 1–3; *St. Mark* 14: 53–72; *St. Luke* 22: 54–71; *St. John* 18: 15–28.)

ACT 10
Judas in Despair

Tableau: Cain, tortured by his conscience, wanders the face of the earth.

(*Genesis* 4: 10–17.)

Scene: Judas, in his shame and despair, hangs himself.

(*St. Matthew* 27: 3–10.)

ACT 11
Christ before Pilate

Scene 1: Christ is driven on by the guards.
Scene 2: The High Council assemble.
Scene 3: Christ is brought before Pilate.
Scene 4: Pilate examines Jesus.
Scene 5: Pilate's wife sends him a message begging him to have no hand in judging Jesus.
Scene 6: Mela tells Pilate that he believes the High Priests to be envious of Jesus.
Scene 7: Pilate finds no fault in Jesus.

(*St. John* 18: 28.)

ACT 12
Christ before Herod

Tableau: The Philistines make sport of Samson.

(*Judges* 16: 25.)

Scene 1: Herod returns Jesus to Pilate.
Scene 2: Jesus is again arraigned before Pilate.
Scene 3: Pilate proposes a choice by the people between Jesus and the murderer Barabbas.
Scene 4: Pilate has Jesus scourged and He is crowned with thorns.

(*St. Luke* 23: 6–11.)

ACT 13
Christ is sentenced to death on the Cross

1st Tableau: Joseph introduced to the people as ruler over Egypt.

(*Genesis* 41: 41.)

2nd Tableau: The sacrifice of a goat as a sin-offering.

(*Numbers* 28: 22.)

Scene 1: The people demand the release of Barabbas.
Scene 2: Pilate delivers up Jesus to be crucified.
(*St. Matthew* 27: 15–26; *St. Mark* 15: 6–15; *St. Luke*
23: 17–26; *St. John* 19: 12–16.)

*Part III of the Passion Play tells of the condemnation
of Christ by Pilate, His death and Resurrection.*

ACT 14
The Way to the Cross

1st Tableau: Isaac, carrying the wood for his own sacrifice,
up Mount Moriah.   (*Genesis* 22: 1–10.)
2nd Tableau: The Israelites look upon the Brazen Serpent
and are cured.   (*Numbers* 21: 8–9.)

Scene 1: Christ carries the cross on the way to Calvary.
Scene 2: Jesus meets His Mother.
Scene 3: Simon of Cyrene is forced to carry the cross.
Scene 4: The women of Jerusalem weep for Jesus.
(*St. Matthew* 27: 32–33; *St. Mark* 15: 21–22; *St. Luke*
23: 26–33; *St. John* 19: 17.)

ACT 15
The Crucifixion

Scene 1: Christ is nailed to the cross.
Scene 2: A spear is thrust into His side.
Scene 3: His body is presented to Joseph of Arimathea.
Scene 4: Christ rests in His Mother's arms.
(*St. Matthew* 27: 34–66; *St. Mark* 15: 23–46; *St. Luke*
23: 36–53; *St. John* 19: 18–42.)

ACT 16
The Resurrection

Scene: Jesus ascends from the tomb.
(*St. Matthew* 28: 1–20; *St. Mark* 16: 1–19; *St. Luke* 24: 1–51;
St. John 20: 1–18.)

CONCLUSION

Hallelujah Chorus
Triumph and Glorification of Christ

11 The 'Tableaux'

The tableaux that precede most of the acts in the Passion Play are designed to remind us that the Passion of Christ was foretold in historical incidents many years earlier.

Indeed, it is said by some, that Christ's submission to His fate was a deliberate act to fulfil the destiny that had been ordained for Him by God and rehearsed for His guidance among the events of the past.

However, though the Passion Play tells in detail the story of that unhappy time, the tableaux do no more than provide a brief reminder of those long gone incidents; they do nothing towards filling in the background for us.

I

The first tableau of importance, in the context of it being a mirror to the future, is that presented before the opening scene in *Act 2*. It shows us the *Sons of Jacob conspiring against their brother, Joseph.*

Jacob had twelve sons, Joseph being the eleventh and the first-born of Rachel—in Jacob's old age.

In consequence of this, and perhaps because of his

mother's over-indulgence, Joseph became something of a pampered favourite with his father; so much so that Jacob's older sons disliked the boy almost from the day of his birth and as he grew up, jealous of the influence he possessed over his father.

As Joseph passed into his middle teens, his brothers' dislike and jealousy swelled up inside them until they actually hated him.

Joseph certainly had a very high opinion of himself, typified in one of many incidents, when he laid claim to be very much a person of outstanding importance. He told four of his brothers that he had dreamed that while they were in the fields binding sheaves of corn, he had seen his sheaf remain erect while their sheaves bowed to his.

Unfortunately the four brothers to whom he boasted of the dream were the sons of Bilhah and Zilpah, hand-maidens to Jacob's first wife, Leah, who felt, as the sons of concubines, less secure than the others.

They told their father of Joseph's dream, but, receiving little sympathy, their hatred for the precocious brother deepened.

Though he was well aware of the hatred he was creating around his own head, Joseph never ceased to offend his brothers; on a subsequent occasion he told them all of a dream he had had in which the sun, the moon and the eleven stars bowed down before him.

It seemed so obvious that the sun symbolized Jacob, the moon Rachel and the eleven stars Jacob's other sons that when the bitterly angry brothers repeated Joseph's story to their father he did rebuke the youth.

But the brothers felt that the reprimand was far less severe than the offence warranted and they went out to the fields in Shechem, to tend Jacob's sheep, deeply incensed and growing more and more angry as they talked the matter over.

Probably aware of the acute resentment of his older sons, Jacob sent Joseph after them to help with the flock, but Joseph failed to catch up with them, nor were they in Shechem when they got there.

A man told the youth that he had seen the eleven brothers walking in the direction of Dothan.

The brothers saw Joseph in the distance as he walked slowly towards them and their anger blazed up. They stood together whispering urgently, determined that they were not going to tolerate the situation any longer. They would kill him.

Then they fell to discussing ways and means of bringing about Joseph's death.

In the action of the scenes that followed this tableau we see the High Priests conspiring against Jesus.

II

Before *Act 5* opens out in the first of its two scenes, the tableau showing *The Manna in the Wilderness* is shown.

The children of Israel came to the wilderness of Sin, that parched, barren and inhospitable region, on the fifteenth day of the second month after they left Egypt.

They were weary beyond belief, ragged and above all, hungry and thirsty. Their mood was one of utter defeat and they began to cry out against their leaders, Moses and Aaron, remembering only the flesh pots of Egypt that they had left so far behind them.

But the Lord appeared to Moses and told him that it would rain bread and that every day thereafter the people could gather up all that they needed and that by the sixth day whatever they had gathered would be doubled.

Moses and Aaron did what they could to convince the

dispirited Israelites of the promise that had been given, but their hopes had been so severely dashed and their physical resources were at such a low ebb that it was difficult to drive home to them the fact that they were not going to be deserted.

The Lord heard the disgruntled murmurings and He spoke again to Moses, assuring him that in the evening they would eat flesh, and in the morning bread.

That same evening a great flock of quails descended onto the camp and in the morning there was a heavy fall of dew.

Even more unbelievably, they found a small, round loaf of bread lying on the ground—and Moses ordered them to take as much of it as they required, regardless of its size. And the tiny loaf proved to be inexhaustible as each of the Israelites in turn broke off all they could eat.

The scene that follows enacts the celebration of the Feast of the Passover by Jesus in company with His disciples.

III

The tableau that precedes the first scene in *Act 6* depicts the stark inhumanity of *Joseph being sold by his twenty pieces of silver.*

It was Reuben, the eldest of the sons of Jacob, who dissuaded his brothers from killing Joseph—but he was nevertheless only too willing to rid their home of one who so persistently claimed to stand out above the rest of them; who even seemed to expect to be worshipped by them.

Reuben agreed with the others that when Joseph did arrive amongst them, that they would cast him into one of the pits that abounded around Dothan; one that was too deep for him to climb out of unaided, and then to abandon him to his fate.

When Joseph did put in a belated appearance, the brothers grabbed him, stripped him of the coat of many colours that had been given to him by his adoring father and threw him into a dry pit. Then they sat down to eat the food they had brought with them and to ponder over the story they should tell Jacob when they returned home.

As they discussed the matter a train of camels, laden with spices, myrrh and other trade-goods, and urged on towards Egypt by its Midianite owners, approached from the direction of Giliad.

Judah, the fourth son of Jacob and as worried as Reuben at the projected murder of Joseph—for he realized that to leave him to die in the pit was as murderous as their original intention to kill him—hit on the idea of selling him to the Midianites. In that way he would be taken to a far land and probably sold again, never to return to his homeland. And in that way too, they would solve the problem of doing away with him without having the sin of murder on their consciences.

Nor had they any difficulty about the transaction—and accepted twenty pieces of silver in exchange for Joseph.

In the first scene that follows, Christ is valued at thirty pieces of silver, and in the second Judas is brought before the Sanhedrin as the man willing to accept such a sum in exchange for betraying Jesus into their hands.

IV

The second of the two tableaux that precedes the action in *Act 7* depicts *Amasa being slain by Joab*.

Joab was commander-in-chief of the forces of King David at the time of the insurrection by the Israelites against him, led by Sheba of Belial. But the men of Judah stayed loyal to their king.

David ordered Amasa to muster his supporters and told him to complete the task within three days, but he took so long about it that it became clear to him that Amasa was deserting to the enemy forces under Sheba.

The king then sent Joab in command of the army in pursuit.

They met at Gibeon and Amasa approached Joab. Joab had a sword hidden under his cloak. The cloak fell open to reveal the weapon but Amasa, not yet aware that Joab suspected him of desertion came right up to Joab and allowed him, apparently in a spirit of friendliness, to take him by the beard, draw his face towards him and to kiss him. And Joab dug his sword into the body of the unsuspecting Amasa.

In scene 4 of this act, Judas betrays his Master with a kiss.

V

The second part of the Passion Play opens with *Act 8*, which, in its turn, is preceded by a tableau showing the *Prophet Micaiah being struck in the face by Ahab*.

Ahab, King of Israel from 873 to 851 B.C., had married Jezebel, daughter of the King of the Zidonians, and she it was who introduced into Israel the idolatrous worship of Baal and the obscene orgies of the Goddess Ashtoreth. And to satisfy her demands, Ahab ordered the persecution of those who continued to worship Jehovah and to kill off all the prophets of the Lord.

But, condemned by the Lord for allowing Jezebel to

give false evidence against Naboth in order that he could take possession of Naboth's vineyards and causing the unfortunate man to be stoned to death, Ahab showed some signs of repentance.

Under Jezebel's influence, Ahab soon returned to his wicked ways, forgot all about the Lord and gave what little devotion he had in him, to Baal again.

War between Israel and Syria was persistent during the reign of King Ahab and then, after three years of uneasy peace, Jehoshaphat, King of Judah, agreed to join Ahab in an attack on Ramoth-Gilead. But first, he was anxious to know if the project had the approval of the Lord.

Ahab gathered no fewer than 400 prophets and demanded to know if the omens were propitious for him to launch an attack on Ramoth-Gilead.

The prophets, to a man, assured both he and King Jehoshaphat that the town would fall into their hands almost before the attack was sent in.

But Jehoshaphat was not so easily satisfied. He was well aware that Jezebel had had all the prophets of the Lord in Israel killed off and that those who were now being consulted were no better than Ahab's *claque*. He demanded that a true prophet of the Lord be found.

Reluctantly Ahab admitted that there was still one prophet of the Lord left in Israel, Micaiah—but he complained bitterly that he hated the man because all his prophecies foretold evil for him.

Jehoshaphat insisted that Micaiah be brought before them.

The two kings seated themselves on their thrones before the entrance to the gate of Samaria and then had all the prophets assembled in front of them. Zedekiah fashioned some horns of iron and prophesied that with them, the joint forces of the two kings would push the Syrians out of Ramoth-Gilead. The other prophets echoed the assurance—and the messengers who had brought Micaiah to the assembly warned him that, as every other prophet had foretold success for the attack, it would be well for him to agree with them.

Micaiah did assure the two kings of their certain success against the Syrians—but, strangely, despite such a favourable prophecy, Ahab warned Micaiah that he must tell nothing but what the Lord had foretold him.

The prophet then admitted that he had been told that the Israelites would be scattered about the hills like sheep without a shepherd.

Angrily, Ahab reminded Jehoshaphat that he could expect no prophecy from Micaiah that would favour any enterprise of his.

Micaiah repeated his prophecy and told the king that the Lord had warned him that all the other prophets would lie.

Zedekiah, the leading personality among the 400 prophets, stepped forward angrily and smacked Micaiah across the face.

Jesus is brought before Annas, in the text of the scenes that follow, and is slapped in the face by Balbus for the manner in which he answered the High Priest.

VI

In one of the two tableaux that open *Act 9*, *Naboth is condemned to death on false evidence.*

Naboth was the owner of a fine vineyard that bordered the palace of King Ahab in Jezreel, but he was too fond of it to sell it to the king.

Jezebel, the notorious wife of Ahab, undertook to get it for him.

She wrote in King Ahab's name to certain of the nobles and elders of Jezreel, proclaiming a fast and ordering them to have Naboth brought before them. She told them to instruct two worthless men to act as witnesses against Naboth, declaring that he had blasphemed both God and the king—and that they should find him guilty and condemn him to be stoned to death.

Similarly, in the act that follows, Jesus is taken before the Sanhedrin and on false evidence He is condemned to death.

VII

The tableaux before *Act 10* is a bitter presentation of *the conscience-stricken Cain: a wanderer on the face of the earth* after killing his brother Abel.

Cain and Abel were the sons of Adam and Eve—the first people to inhabit the earth.

Cain offered some of the fruit of the earth to God, but the Lord seemed to prefer the animal sacrificed for Him by Abel.

Angry and bitter at the refusal of his offer, Cain quarrelled with his brother, and the argument grew so fierce and hysterical that he over-reached himself, and almost before he knew what he had done, he had killed Abel.

Cain was still recovering from the shock when the Lord appeared to him and asked him where his brother was.

He professed not to know and demanded, bitterly, "Am I my brother's keeper?"

Understanding what had happened, God cursed Cain and warned him that never again would the ground yield a harvest for him and that he would become a vagabond and a fugitive on the face of the world.

Cain cried out that the punishment was more than he could bear, but, stricken by conscience and with every man's hand against him, he became a hapless wanderer and a lost soul.

The single scene of Act 10 plays out the story of Judas Iscariot as, torn by remorse, the disciple goes out beyond the city walls of Jerusalem and finds a tree on which to hang himself.

VIII

The tableau that precedes the first scene of *Act 12* depicts the blinded *Samson being treated as a figure of scorn* as he is put on exhibition before the Philistines.

Samson, one of the judges of Israel, was a notoriously passionate man, born with the super-natural strength that allowed him to indulge it to the full.

On one occasion, in an act of revenge for the loss of his Philistine wife, he caught 300 jackals, tied burning torches to their tails and sent them into the cornfields of his father-in-law to destroy them; on another he allowed himself to be handed over to the Philistines as a captive, then once he was among them, he snapped his bonds, seized the jawbone of an ass and with it killed more than 1,000 of them.

Yet he fell in love with another Philistine, Delilah. Beautiful and with a tremendous personality, she was yet mean, treacherous and a Philistine among Jews.

Her countrymen found no difficulty in bribing her to discover wherein lay her husband's superhuman strength, and for a large enough sum she was quite prepared to curb it as soon as she found out how, so that he could be taken as a captive.

But three times she failed to uncover Samson's secret as he fobbed her off with untruths. She was persistent, very persuasive and apparently a devoted wife—and in the end Samson told her that if his hair was cut short he would be reduced to the strength of a normal man.

Delilah soothed Samson into a deep sleep and quietly cut off his hair.

Waking, Samson knew that his strength had gone, that God had forsaken him and that he was now, at last, about to fall into the hands of the Philistines.

He was bound with chains, his eyes were put out and he was sent to Gaza and imprisoned there.

The long days dragged by in the darkness of the blind, in the dankness of a stone prison and in the helpless dismay of being so heartlessly betrayed by Delilah—until, on the Feast of Dagon, his captors remembered him and resolved to bring him out to enliven the celebrations.

Samson was dragged out of his dungeon and compelled to act the blind buffoon before 3,000 delighted, jeering spectators in the temple of Dagon and an even greater multitude that clung to every pinnacle and roof that overlooked the courtyard.

In the action of the play there is enacted here, the dreadful episode of the scourging of Christ and of His crowning with a crown of thorns for the entertainment of the crowds.

IX

The first of the two tableaux that precedes *Act 14* take the form of a presentation of *Isaac carrying the wood up Mount Moriah* on which he is to be sacrificed.

God ordered Abraham to take his son, Isaac, with him to

the land of Moriah—three days journey from Beersheba where they lived—and there, on one of the mountain peaks, he was tó sacrifice the youth as a burnt offering.

Abraham rose early on the following morning, saddled his ass and, taking two of his young men and Isaac his son with him, he cut sufficient wood to build the fire for the sacrifice. They loaded the timber on to the ass, lashed it down and headed for Moriah.

When they arrived there, Abraham chose Mount Moriah as the place for the sacrifice and at its foot he halted his little party and instructed the two young men to wait for him there with the animal.

He unloaded the beast and gave the kindling wood to Isaac to carry up the mountainside, for his pyre.

A heartrending scene follows of the pitiable journey made by Christ, bearing His cross through the streets of Jerusalem towards Calvary and His crucifixion.

12 Personalities of the Play

The names of many of the citizens of Oberammergau recur again and again over the years in the history of the Passion Play. Some of them became, in their day, famous actors, others assumed the responsible duties of directing and producing the plays, while still others composed the musical scores or wrote the texts.

Each of them, in his own way, took a leading part in honouring the vow that was made so solemnly by their forebears in 1633.

Many thousands more of them, though bearing the same illustrious names, have passed unnoticed, having performed less important roles, given of their music in the annonymity of the orchestra pit, or—and let no one forget them—are those who made the production of the plays possible as carpenters, scene-shifters and in many another craft.

Indeed, only the name of one man stands out in the story of Oberammergau for doing nothing for which the community could be either proud of him, or grateful to him: Kasper Schisler, the village labourer, who carried the plague on his person, from the outside world into that tiny hamlet and so condemned probably more than half the population to a horrible death.

Yet, 300 years later, there is little thought of censure for the long dead man; people merely shrug their shoulders sympathetically at the mention of his name. They realize that no one today can possibly understand the heartaches and temptations to which a man could be subject, exiled, from his family whilst all around him the ravages of the Black Death was reaping its dread toll.

In those days of no telephones, no mail, and, in the midst of pestilence, forbidden any form of communication beyond his immediate neighbourhood, what must have been the state of his mind as he wondered desperately how his wife and children were faring only three or four short miles away, down in the valley? Surely the temptation to go to them and, with his strong arms about them, to stand four-square together with them to face whatever was to be must not have been tremendous.

What would any one of us have done in such a situation?

But Kaspar Schisler takes no further part in this story—he and the whole of his family were consigned to the death pits in 1632, leaving no Oberammergauer to carry his name into the future.

Wraiths peep out at us from the distant past without feature or substance, but leaving some contribution towards the Passion Play behind them. Sebastian Wild, for instance, an Augsburg Mastersinger of the sixteenth century, must be given a great deal of credit for one of the earlier versions of the play. Johann Albl, the parish priest of Weilheim, whose play was performed as early as 1600—the text of which was almost certainly interwoven with that of Sebastian Wild by the earliest producers of the Oberammergau Plays; and the five members of the Rutz family who took part in the sixth season in 1680; Jakob as John, Antoni as Pilate, Joseph as Caiaphas and Viet and Sebastian in minor roles.

Reaching forward to the other end of the chronological

scale, the name that claims out attention as the outstanding personality connected with the Passion Play today is that of Georg Johann Lang, probably the most famous of all the long line of directors.

Lang was born in Oberammergau in 1889, and his first venture into the Passion Play occurred in 1900 when he took a walk-on part as a boy actor. A decade later, at the age of 21, he was elected stage manager, and in time for the 1922 season he was given charge of the whole production.

With this experience behind him and helped by his brother Raimund—later to become burgomaster of Oberammergau—Georg Lang modernized the stage in readiness for the 1930 season.

He continued to direct the play during the 1934 tercentenary season and again, after the Second World War, in 1950. In 1959 Lang was awarded, by the Community of Oberammergau, a badge of honour as a token of their profound gratitude. And in this, his eighty-first year, he was once again elected to direct a Season of Passion Plays.

It is noteworthy that a member of the Lang family held the post of Director of the Play from 1880 forward.

The part of Christ was played by Jakob Zwink during the broken season of 1800/1801, with such conspicuous success that he was again elected to play the role in 1811 and again in 1815—and yet again in 1820. But that was not to be the end of his career on the Passion Play stage. Giving up the tremendously emotional role of Christ, Jacob Zwink took up the lesser, though by no means unimportant part, of Peter, for both the 1830 and 1840 seasons.

Tobias Flunger played the part in 1850. Rupert Schauer followed in 1860, and the so-successful Joseph Mayr carried the part during the seasons 1870, 1880, and 1890.

Anton Lang created a brilliant reputation for himself as Jesus Christ in 1900 and was re-elected to the part in both 1910 and 1922.

Alois Lang played the part in 1930 and again in the tercentenary year of 1934. Born in 1891, he started, as so many others did in Oberammergau, as a woodcarver. He took his first part in the Passion Play as Joseph, in one of the tableaux, in 1910 at the age of 19. In 1922 he played the role of Nathaniel and understudied the part of Christ. After his two season's run as Christ, Alois Lang was not forgotten; he appeared again as the Prologue in 1950 and as Simon of Bethany in 1960.

Anton (Toni) Preisinger carried the part with gentle sincerity in 1950, and there was no doubt about his re-election for the 1960 season. Born in 1912, he made his first appearance on the Passion Play stage as an angel in a tableau, in 1922 and followed that with a similar performance in 1930. He played the role of Lazarus in 1934, his first speaking part, and understudied the Apostle John at the same time. Preisinger owns and operates the 400-year-old Alte Poste Hotel, an inn of some importance in the market place of Oberammergau.

Judas the betrayer was portrayed by Johann Lechner in 1815 and was followed by his son, another Johann Lechner in 1820, 1830 and 1840, and it seemed that the Lechner's were irreplaceable when another of the same family, Gregor Lechner, continued the tradition by enacting this searching part in 1850, 1860, 1870 and again in 1880. So successfully did Gregor assume the character of Judas that, on more than one occasion, a few members of the audience lost control over their emotions and pelted him with stones as he passed through the streets of Oberammergau in his robes and beard, on his way to lunch during the interval.

Johann Zwink played this so difficult role in 1890, 1900 and 1910, after playing the less onerous part of John during the seasons of 1870 and 1880. During 1910 Johann Zwink was joined on the stage by his daughter, Ottilie, who took the part of Mary in that season.

Guido Mayr was the Judas of 1922 and 1930, and then, once again, a son followed in his father's footsteps.

Johann Zwink, son of the Johann Zwink who had taken the part at the turn of the century, played Judas during the tercentenary year of 1934.

Hans Schwaighofer, born in 1920, was cast as one of the crowd for the 1930 season and, being very much of a musician, played in the orchestra during the 1934 season— at 14 years of age. He took the role of Judas in both 1950 and 1960 and doubled as deputy producer to the famous Georg Lang. Like so many who were at one time or another with the Passion Play, Schwaighofer studied at the Oberammergau School of Woodcarving and later at the Academy of Fine Arts in Munich. He is now a teacher in the village school.

Lang was the name of every Mary, Mother of Jesus, in the years 1830, 1840 and 1850. Rosa Lang, who took the part in 1890 with distinction, never married and died in a convent.

Ottilie Zwink, daughter of Johann, the Judas from 1890 to 1910, took the part in 1910.

Anni Rutz, who played Mary during the seasons 1930 and 1934, was generally considered to be perhaps the finest actress ever to appear on the Passion Play stage, but, unfortunately, though she was still unmarried at the time of the election of the cast for the abortive 1940 season, she was approaching her fortieth birthday—and beyond the age limit traditionally laid down for feminine roles in the Oberammergau Passion Play.

Anneliese Mayr took the part in 1950. Irmi Dengg followed her in 1960.

Mary Magdalene, the more important of the only two principal feminine roles in the play, though it is the Madonna who receives the kudos, was enacted by Therese Rutz in 1815. She was a descendant of the Rutz who took the part of John in the early Passion Play of 1680.

Viktoria Rutz played the role in 1840. Helena Lang succeeded her in 1850, Josepha Lang carried on through 1860 and 1870 and was followed by Maria Lang in 1880. A Mayr filled the role in 1910 and was followed by Paula Rendl in 1922.

Johanna Preisinger, the sister of Anton Preisinger the Christ of the 1950 and 1960 seasons, took the part of Mary Magdalene in 1930, to be followed by another member of the Mayr family, Clare Mayr, in the tercentenary year of 1934. Gabriele Gropper succeeded her in 1950 and then, yet again a Mayr.

Anneliese Mayr, followed in 1960 after spending the previous season in the slightly less important role of Mary.

The part of John, the apostle, is first recorded as having been played by Jakob Rutz in 1680, and on that same occasion no fewer than four others of the Rutz family took part in that very early Passion Play.

In later years the Bierling family seemed to take charge of the role, playing it first during the seasons of 1830, 1840 and 1850.

Johann Zwink played the part in 1870 and 1880, in later years to become an outstanding Judas.

Peter Rendl enacted the part of John in 1900, followed by Melchior Bierling in 1910 and 1922 and Johann Lang in 1930.

Melchior Bierling returned to the part for the tercentenery year of 1934.

Martin Margold broke the hold of the Bierlings on the part of John, once again, though he was understudied by Werner Bierling, who renewed the family connection in 1960.

Peter, the 'best loved apostle', was enacted by Jakob Zwink in 1830 and 1840, after an exhausting four seasons in the role of Christ.

A Rendl took the part in 1900, followed by Andreas Lang, a noted performer of the part during the seasons of 1910 and 1922. Peter Rendl took over in 1930 and started the 1934 season. Unfortunately he died in the middle of it and Hubert Mayr had to take over the part for the rest of the run.

Hugo Rutz played Peter in 1950 at the age of 64. He had acted the role of Caiaphas in 1922, 1930 and 1934.

Hans Maier was elected the Peter of the 1960 season. Having an excellent bass voice he had been in the choirs of 1930 and 1934, leading it in 1950.

The role of Annas was another example of how one of the older families of Oberammergau seem to have made a particular role their own peculiar province.

Jakob Rutz held the part during the seasons of 1800, 1811 and 1815, and was followed by Franz Rutz in 1830. Another Franz Rutz took the part in 1890.

Sebastian Lang, father of the famous director Georg Johann Lang and his brother Burgomaster Raimund Lang, took the part in 1910 and 1922.

Anton Lechner played the part in both 1930 and during the tercentenery year of 1934. He had been a drawing master in Oberammergau and started his long career in Passion Plays as a 'Child of Adam' in the 1870 season. He was to continue to take various roles in the play until 1950, when he was 88 years of age. He died in the following year.

Jakob Klucker, yet another of those who had been pupils at the Oberammergau State School of Woodcarving enacted the part in the 1950 and 1960 seasons.

The role of Caiaphas, the High Priest, is recorded as having been performed by Joseph Rutz as early as 1680, the year in which five of that family appeared on the stage at the same time.

Peter Lang had a long run in the role during the 1800/1 season and those of 1811, 1815, and 1820, before taking over the directorship of the play in 1830.

Jakob Mayr, father of the famous 'Christ' of the 1870–1890 era, played the part of Caiaphas in 1840 and 1850.

Johann Lang succeeded Mayr in the role in 1860 and held it continuously until after the 1890 season. He was at one time burgomaster of Oberammergau.

Hugo Rutz held it during the seasons 1922, 1930 and 1934.

Benedikt Stückl, son of the Benedikt who played Nathaniel in 1930, portrayed Caiaphas in 1950, but he broke his thigh in a ski-ing accident in 1960, just three months before he was due to take the part for the second time. Stückl was at one time chef at the famous Alte Poste Hotel in Oberammergau, owned by Anton Preisinger but he now owns his own hostelry in the village, called the 'Zur Rose'.

The part of Pontius Pilate was played by Antoni Rutz in 1680, Modest Stückl in 1850, Rendl during the years 1880 and 1890, Bauer in 1900 and 1910.

Hans Mayr, the Herod of a decade earlier, played the part of Pilate in 1922, before returning to his earlier role in 1934.

Melchior Breitsamter took over the season of 1930, was re-elected in the same part for the tercentenery year of 1934 and continued in it during 1950 and 1960.

Readers will have noticed how certain of the older families of Oberammergau seem to have monopolized the senior roles in the Passion Play—understandably, as it was their ancestors chiefly, who took the vow in 1633, pledging them to the task.

The Langs stand out in this respect—though the first of the family of that name did not come to Oberammergau until 1723. Yet, by 1770, they had acquired so much influence in the community that it was one of them who was called upon to intercede with the Elector Maximilian Joseph in the hope of persuading him to lift the ban placed by him on the public performance of religious plays.

Forty years later, in 1810, his son Georg was given the task of making a similar plea to Maximilian II.

Fifteen of the Langs took speaking parts in the play during the ninteenth and twentieth centuries, holding each of them for one or more seasons; four of the family have directed the play, and very many more of that name have taken part in one or other of the host of minor roles.

A sister of Ludwig Lang, who directed the plays in 1900 and 1910, headed the team of wardrobe mistresses for forty years—adding her skill to the service the Langs have rendered to the Passion Play for over 250 years.

Members of the Zwink family too, have performed zealously in the same undertaking, as have the Rutz, Mayr, Bierling and many another family, regarding the fulfilment of the vow as an inescapable duty.

None of them has forgotten that he had at least one ancestor who attended that service of intercession in the village church over 300 years ago; most of them recall, too, that the names of Albl, Rutz, Zwink, Stückl, among others, appear in the parish register of deaths for the years 1632 and 1633, as having died of the plague—and whose bones lie buried alongside the miserable Kasper Schisler, in one of the mass graves in the little cemetery so very near their homes.

The 1970 performances of the Passion Play included among the players, Helmut Fischer and Gregor Breitsamter who shared the role of Christ – and the part of Mary was played alternately by Beatrix Lang and Irmi Dengg. Fräulein Dengg had taken the same part during the season of 1960 and by her fine acting had assured her re-election to that role in 1970. She also played Martha during 1970.

Among other notable performers during the 1970 season, Martin Wagner and Toni Maderspacher both enacted the role of Judas; Hermann Haser and Werner Härtle, Peter – and Rolf Zigon and Vitus Zwink, John. Zwink also played Lazarus. Willy Bierling took the part of Joseph of Arimathea and the role of Mary Magdalene was shared by Christl Rutz and Elisabeth Jablonka.

Max Jablonka and Arthur Haser played the High Priest, Caiaphas; Martin Magold and Zeno Bierling, Pilate – and Herod was portrayed in turn by Benedikt Stückl Sen. and Otto Wunder.

The Play of 1970 was produced by Anton Preisinger, his deputy being Jakob Klucker and his assistant, Hans Maier Jun. It was stage managed by Rupert Breitsamter Sen. and the musical director was Werner Zimmermann. The orchestra of some sixty-five instrumentalists was conducted at one time or another by Werner Zimmermann, Ulrich Hochenleitner and Hans Gotzler, and the choir-master, Hans Gotzler, directed a choir of forty-eight singers.

13 Training Plays

Though the rehearsals for the Passion Play start no more than a year in advance of the season and the casting in the September of the previous year, there is never any total cessation of activity between one season and the next—a decade apart.

At the end of any season of Passion Plays, performed before more than half-a-million spectators, many weeks of hard work are needed in which to 'clean up'.

Repairs have to be made to damaged seats, wall panelling, carpets, electric wiring and the multiplicity of other things that suffer from wear and tear during a hectic season. Then the whole structure of the vast theatre must be made weather-proof, pest-free and secure against the long years when it is little used.

All the thousands of costumes, props and the scenery need to be repaired, repainted and refurbished—and stowed away among the recesses of the great store rooms —moth-free, damp-proof, safe from light-fingered souvenir hunters and in such order that each item, when it is again required, can be located almost with the ease of finding a number in a telephone directory.

The office staff has much to do in clearing up a heavy

back-log of correspondence, in meeting all the financial obligations incurred in staging such an enormous production and in closing the accounts with tour organizations, travel companies and ticket agencies.

And, perhaps most urgent of all the actors who, after six months of full-time profitless employment in the great theatre, must again find jobs for themselves and the means of earning a living; the young girls who had deliberately abstained from marriage so that they would be eligible to take part in the play, need to look around for husbands—unless they hope to be chosen again, ten years hence—and the many children, who have had their season as actors, must again return to full-time schooling.

Even the hoteliers must set themselves to receive a different kind of guest—holidaymakers, sightseers and tourists, rather than those who had come to sink themselves into the atmosphere of a solemn, historical occasion, to see one of the greatest plays on earth, or, in their fashion, to worship God.

True, the bustle in and around the Passion Theatre will slowly quieten as the months go by, but already the director will be planning ahead. Suggestions for alterations to the text and the music will need to be considered—not casually, as with some musical revue, but with care for historical accuracy, attention to the purpose of the play, for the solemnity of its presentation—and with reverence.

Improvements to the theatre and its facilities must be decided long in advance of the next season; building repairs, modernization, box office facilities, lighting and seating—and, once again, as the years drift by, all the problems of publicity, of the allocation of seats, the prices to be charged, the transport facilities, accommodation, the number of performances to be given, and a host of other details must be discussed, agreed—and carried into effect.

Then too, the hoteliers and the restaurateurs must prepare for the massive wave of expected guests and visitors, the souvenir shops will be redecorated and restocked, the church pews polished, and the printers will be inundated with calls to prepare programmes, tickets, scripts, street guides and hotel brochures. Allocations of seats must be made to travel organizations, tour companies and private clubs; railways, airlines and bus operators will revise their schedules, village gardens will be completely replanted and the religious frescoes on the walls of the houses and buildings, repainted—all this and much more besides, in a fast growing tide of preparation for the new season.

But there can be no 'easing off' for the actors; almost without pause, during the whole of the decade between seasons, they must practise their art. Experienced players need to broaden their abilities, future performers have to be given the opportunity to learn how to act, hopefuls must be given their chance to feel their feet on a stage in front of an audience—even children must be encouraged to step out before a vast and crowded auditorium.

For, as always, when the election for the cast of the next season's play is held, only those who are Oberammergauans will be eligible. None will be brought in from outside the village, no professional actors will be engaged—not even a producer from beyond the boundaries of Oberammergau will be asked either for advice or assistance.

The musicians must rehearse constantly too, the producers need actors to practise on, scene-painters cannot neglect their craft and even the stage-hands have to practise the technique of changing a scene in the shortest possible space of time and with the least fuss.

Long ago it was obvious to the members of the Play Committee that it was becoming necessary to stage 'training plays' throughout the 'between' years so that the citizens of Oberammergau could gain experience, improve their performances and develop their talents.

As far back as 1748 a 'serial' play was produced in the village, entitled, *Die Kreuzschule*—the Sufferings of Christ; designed so that a single act of the play was presented each Sunday during Lent.

In that first year, between the Passion seasons of 1740 and 1750, the play was produced and performed in the village church, but ten years later the production was so successful that it had to be transferred to the open square, where more people could see and enjoy each act in the drama.

In those early years *Die Kreuzschule* was performed during Lent, two years in advance of each Passion season, but later it was moved to the middle of the 'between' years—1785 and 1795. And so it continued until it made its final appearance in 1905—each 'series' proving itself to be a veritable cradle for talent and an immensely successful precursor to the Passion Play itself.

Die Kreuzschule was a strange play and was often referred to as the 'umgekehrte Passion'—the Passion Play in reverse; for it was precisely that. While the Passion Play proper told of Christ's sufferings and was supported, between the acts, by tableaux portraying incidents from the Old Testament that paralleled the story of Christ's passion, *Die Kreuzschule* told the Old Testament stories in play form and interspersed the acts with tableaux of the various stages in Christ's passion—an age-old foretelling of the events that overtook Jesus of Nazareth.

The training value of that serial play and the wide interest that was taken in it, encouraged the producer to experiment with others. In 1716 a play based on the life of St. Hermenegild was performed at Whitsuntide, telling the story of how the saint, a son of the Visigoth King, embraced Christianity, headed a revolt against the powerful Byzantines, and when he lost the battle refused to abandon his faith and was executed.

So deeply was the audience intrigued by it that it was repeated twice, and on one of these occasions it was performed before Bernard, the Abbot of Ettal, who, so we are told, expressed himself as being "greatly honoured" by the event.

From about 1850 Alois Daisenberger, the parish priest of Oberammergau, wrote a whole series of plays to be performed by members of his congregation. In them he broke new ground, adding spice and variety to the productions by using historical themes as the subject of many of his dramas—though he by no means neglected the traditional type of religious plays.

In 1860 these plays were staged in the annex of the Passion Play Theatre, among the dressing rooms and store rooms, and became an important part of the 'build-up' towards the Passion seasons.

In these surroundings—and perhaps because of the fast rising fame of the Passion Plays, far beyond the narrow confines of the Ammer Valley—there occurred a sharp upsurge in the demand for parts in the Passion Play from the villagers, and as the 'between seasons' plays were the only source of learning, and indeed were being used as 'try-outs' for the players, it became urgently necessary to increase the frequency of such productions.

Other playwrights began to write material especially for production in Oberammergau between the Passion seasons —and a number of them achieving some fame in their day. Richard Voss, for instance, settled down in nearby Berchtesgaden and gathered a sufficient reputation from his writings to be appointed librarian to the Wartburg by the Duke of Weimar. Unfortunately, ill-health cut his career short, and he died at Köngsee in 1918.

Others included Hartl-Mitius, Herman von Schmid, Benno Rauchenegger—and the never-to-be-forgotten Ludwig Anzengruber, an Austrian who created something of a furore with his anti-clerical play, *Der Pfarrer von Kirchfeld.* His play *Der Meineidbauer* was performed in Oberammergau in 1890, the year after his death.

By 1901 it was obvious that there was a very real need for a properly equipped theatre in which to stage these 'interim' plays—the stage of the Passion Theatre was much too large and the annex far too inconvenient. In that year the Kleines Theatre—the Little Theatre was built and opened. It stood opposite the town hall, seated some 400 people in comfort and offered a 'proper' stage and auditorium to players and playgoers alike.

Yet by 1930 the variety of organizations in Oberammergau were crowding one another for play dates during which they could stage their own productions—almost swamping the official plays. Clubs, associations, social circles and play groups all clamoured for their turn in the Kleines Theatre—and all of them, including the oldest of them all, the Lukas or Wood-carvers Club, began to take their place in the calendar as viable training plays.

Outstanding perhaps, among the many brilliant plays staged in the Kleines Theatre during the years that followed, was Weismantel's *Die Pestnot Anno 1633*—The Plague of 1633—performed during the years 1933, 1949 and revived for the third time in 1958.

Plays began to be performed that claimed precedence at certain times of the year; nativity plays were staged at Christmas; Easter of course, Whitsuntide and on saints days.

Among a host of such plays presented during the

'interim' years of the present century, it is only possible to recall a few of the better known. A folk drama, *Das Wunder des heiligen Florian*—The Miracle of St. Florian, Max Dingler's *Das Judasspiel*—the Judas Play, and *Das Weib des Jephta*—Jephta's Wife, by Lissauer.

Two plays by Alois Johannes Lippl were presented on the stage of the Kleines Theatre: *Totentanz*—Dance of Death, and *Die Pfingstorgel*—The Whitsuntide Organ. Others included Hugin's *Ernte*—Harvest, *Birnbush und Hollerstauden*—The Peartree and the Elderbush, by Joseph Maria Lutz, and of course, Siegmund Graff's *Die Heimkehr des Matthias Bruck*—The Homecoming of Matthias Bruck.

It will be seen even from this limited selection of productions that there arose a distinct tendency to interpose secular plays among the religious dramas, newly written plays with those that were first produced 200 and 300 years earlier, comedies with tragedies and simple stories vied with large-scale productions for their place on the stage of the Little Theatre. And, as time went by, these performances were so varied in their character that they did a great more than serve as training plays—they attracted a much wider audience, kept the interest of the regular playgoers alive and, in fact, became a rich source of entertainment that was appreciated far beyond the Ammergau.

But no success, however brilliant, owed anything to professional actors. As in the Passion Play itself, every actor, every stage-hand and every set-designer was an amateur and a citizen of Oberammergau. They received no payment for their services and had to do a full day's work to earn a living before they could either settle down to study a part, or to step out on to the stage of the Kleines Theatre.

Indeed, the only immediate reward was the 'party' that invariably followed each 'last' performance and was given to the actors, producers, designers, stage-hands and everybody else who had helped in the production. Always it would be held in some inn in the neighbourhood, and there would be singing, dancing and drinking until the early hours of the next morning.

And for those who took part there was the satisfaction of knowing that they had taken the opportunity to learn to act, to widen their experience or to enhance their reputation as actors—and, above all, that in so doing had performed under the eyes of the members of the committee that would, in due time, 'elect' the cast for the Passion Play.

14 Epilogue

And as so often happens, towards the end of the performance during the late afternoon of a summer's day, thunder begins to rumble around the mountain-girt valley until, above and around the vast open-air proscenium, lightning begins to slash and flare at the mountain peaks—to form a fiery backdrop to the scene of Christ on the Cross.

Index